The Young Actor's
Book of Improvisation

The Young Actor's Book of Improvisation

DRAMATIC SITUATIONS FROM
SHAKESPEARE TO SPIELBERG

AGES 7–11

Sandra Caruso
with
Susan Kosoff

HEINEMANN
Portsmouth, NH

Heinemann
A division of Reed Elsevier Inc.
361 Hanover Street
Portsmouth, NH 03801-3912
Offices and agents throughout the world

Several of Lowell Swortzell's plays are the basis of improvisations in this book.

Library of Congress Cataloging-in-Publication Data
Caruso, Sandra.
    The young actor's book of improvisation : Dramatic situations from Shakespeare to Spielberg : ages 7–11 / Sandra Caruso with Susan Kosoff.
        p.   cm.
    Includes bibliographical references and index.
    Summary: A sourcebook of techniques designed to develop improvisational skills in young actors.
    ISBN 0-325-00048-4 (alk. paper)
    1. Improvisation (Acting)–Juvenile literature. [1. Plays–Improvisation. 2. Acting–Technique.] I. Kosoff, Susan, 1943– . II. Title.
PN2071.I5C272   1998
792'.028–dc21   97–50420
                                                                       CIP
                                                                        AC

Editor: Lisa A. Barnett
Cover design: Barbara Werden
Manufacturing: Courtney Ordway

Printed in the United States of America on acid-free paper
02 01 00 99 98   DA   1 2 3 4 5 6 7 8 9

Improvisation vanishes, which makes it unique—
a kiss, a sunset, a dance, a joke—
none will ever return in quite the same way.
Each happens only once in the history of the universe.
                          Stephen Nachmanovitch

To my sweet husband, Dee Caruso
My dear parents, Tom and Helen Maley
My wonderfully bizarre brother, Tim, his wife, Eileen,
   and my special niece, Chloe
My sister-in-law, Dorothy James
and all my dogs, past and present
                          Sandra Caruso

To my Eliot Street family
Amanda, Andi, Sue
and—of course—Emily, who is love
                          Susan Kosoff

CONTENTS

FOREWORD

THE MANY MEANINGS OF IMPROVISATION

Remember that moment in *Alice's Adventures in Wonderland* when the March Hare admonishes Alice to say what she means? "I do," she hastily replies, but, after pausing, adds, "at least I mean what I say—that's the same thing, you know" (Carroll 1965, 68–69).

But is it? The Mad Hatter doesn't seem to think so: "Not the same thing a bit. Why, you might just as well say that 'I see what I eat' is the same thing as 'I eat what I see'" (Carroll 1965, 174). And he does have a point, doesn't he? Words can mean many things, and we may mean many different things even as we speak them. But we can't be like Humpty Dumpty, who scornfully tells Alice that when he uses a word it means exactly what he chooses it to mean, neither more nor less. Well, we all know what happened to him!

Actors, perhaps better than anyone else, recognize the importance of knowing the meanings of words. They first must find the significance of every line of dialogue and then determine how to make that meaning clear in the ways they speak, move, and gesture. Often they go well beyond this stage to *become* the meaning, as they actually display a sense of fear, hope, or whatever emotional state they may be playing. Pinocchio, after his long and sometimes painful discovery of the meaning of truth, eventually becomes a real boy, the personification of honesty and the very meaning of his character.

Improvisation is an actor's most effective tool for discovering the exact meanings of their character's words and behavior. It allows actors to respond in as many different actions as they need to find the one that seems to them the most correct for the moment, for the scene, and for the play. And no matter how experienced they may be or how many awards they may have won, most performers depend on improvisation to develop each new role and each new situation they play on stage or on film. It is at the heart of their craft and essential to yours as well, whether you are taking acting classes, preparing to appear in a play, or just reading a script at home for the fun of it.

But what is it, exactly? The word *improvisation* contains different meanings and offers several possible challenges to readers of this book. One definition, according to my dictionary, is the "invention" or "composition" of something from available materials; in other words, it means to make something out of the things around us. In the case of acting, this "something" is a character made from two kinds of available materials: a story or situation (the script or idea) and ourselves (the performers). The challenge for actors is to bring these two together and make them one. And that, as you are about to discover in the many opportunities that await you here, is what you do when you follow the process of response and reaction that is the essence of improvisation.

My dictionary goes on to say that *improvisation* also may mean "to foresee" or "to provide." To be sure, when we improvise we are doing both of these at the same time: we are foreseeing a conclusion for the scene by responding to some basic questions. What are the situations in which the characters find themselves? What can they do to work their way out of or through these circumstances? How can they gain what they want in life? Or from each other? What will happen if they do? What will happen if they don't? By reacting to these questions, we discover the motivation of our characters and the behavior that defines their identity; this exploration through action provides the meaning of what they say and do.

Another dictionary agrees that *improvisation* signifies to utter or to perform *extempore*, impromptu, or on the spur of the moment. This definition includes a valuable phrase we should keep in mind as we use this book. When we improvise, it says, we "provide for the occasion." I can't think of a better motto for a class or workshop in improvisation, because that is exactly what we do each time we perform. Through our actions we provide the occasion by defining it, by making it happen, and by seeming to experience it. Once our character speaks with our voice, moves with our movement, and takes on aspects of our personality, it and the occasion begin to merge and to belong to us.

Another definition says that *improvisation* also means to recite or to make something offhand or to perform spontaneously. But beware, for then the dictionary adds two words that are dangerous to actors: *without preparation*. This thought makes me madder than the Mad Hatter, for I firmly believe that this is not the same thing, not a bit! In improvisation there *must be* preparation! However quick and spontaneous actors may seem to be, their words and actions come from their knowledge of situations and from their intuition to pursue appropriate directions in developing them. Preparation for improvisation is *exactly* what this book is all about, offering the background information and basic ingredients you need to act out the lives of your characters. Read each selection carefully and you will be prepared to respond—ready to improvise!

One also can see the word *improve* lurking inside the word *improvise,* and that is yet another challenge lurking inside the pages of this book. It gives us the opportunity to take these characters and stories and find solutions that in some cases may be quite different from those in the original sources. Part of the fun in improvising a scene is going back to see the actual outcomes in the plays, novels, and films from which they are taken. Comparing our solution with those of others can be enlightening, especially when they prove to be quite different. And it's always a nice feeling when we think our personal solution improves on the original, as sometimes happens.

By improvising, you may seize the exciting situations and dynamic characters you meet here and go anywhere you want with them, make them say and do what you think they should, and have them become your friends or, better still, part of yourself.

Yes, these are a lot of meanings for one little word to contain, I agree. But be prepared to detect many more as you proceed through these pages. For improvisation, by its very nature, keeps acquiring new life and finding new meanings to stimulate our imaginations and to energize our creative reflexes. It's a word so alive that it refuses to stand still or to stay quiet for very long, and it's waiting here for you to tell it what to do next!

So put it to work now and discover where improvisation can take you and where your responses can deliver it. You soon will recognize that you are acting better, and with deeper meaning, than ever before.

Happy improvising!

ACKNOWLEDGMENTS

My thanks to all my acting teachers—Sanford Meisner, Lee Strasberg, Uta Hagen, Charles Conrad, Jeff Corey, Estelle Harman, Howard Storm, Charles Nelson Reily, Michael Shurtleff, and Milton Katselas—as well as to my inspiring colleagues and students in the School of Theater, Film and Television at UCLA. For suggesting material, special thanks to Deirdre Grace Callanan, high school English teacher; Christine Coker, UCLA student; Orlin Corey, Anchorage Press; Maggie Nolan Donovan, teacher; Ursula Ferro, Child Development Consultant; Hanay Geiogamah, faculty, Playwriting and Native American Studies, School of Theater, Film and Television, UCLA; Krista Harrison, high school student; Pat Harter, professor, School of Theater, Film and Television, UCLA; Ina Levin, Editorial Project Manager, Teacher Creative Materials; Michael Levin, high school English teacher; Dr. Susan Popkin Mach, Adolescent and Young Adult Literature, UCLA; Helen Maley, Associate Professor, Early Childhood Education, Wheelock College; Gay Nelson, Children's Librarian, West Tisbury Library, Martha's Vineyard, Massachusetts; Beverly Robinson, professor, School of Theater, Film and Television, UCLA; Lowell Swortzell, professor, Educational Theater, New York University; Edit Villarreal, Vice Chair, School of Theater, Film and Television, UCLA, faculty, playwriting and Chicano studies; Laura Wessel, Anchorage Press. Thanks to Cella, Florence Street Elementary School, and Peter Lecouras, Fremont High School in Los Angeles, for allowing me to test some of the improvisations in their classrooms. Thanks to Adam de la Pena for assistance in film research on the web.

SANDRA CARUSO

Thank you to Betty Bobp, who urged me, in her inimitable fashion, to work with Sandra Caruso on this book, and to Sandra for her gracious invitation to join her on the project. Heartfelt thanks to Marjorie and Harald Bakken, Martha Bakken, Debbie Grozen Bieri, Maggie and Edward

Donovan, Kay Arden Elliott, Priscilla Fales and Liz Moore, Laura and
Michael Garand, Jesse and Bee, Jeffrey Kosoff, Melissa and Alan Miller,
Barbara Phillips, Hanna Schneider, Betsy and Ray Schoen, Jane Staab, and
the Wheelock Family Theatre for helping me get from there to here, and
to Becky Thompson, my north star in the journey.

SUSAN KOSOFF

We extend our sincere gratitude to Vicky Bijur, our literary agent; Kay
Arden Elliott, our editorial coordinator and researcher; and Arthur Leigh,
our editor.

Introduction

Improvisation is at the heart of human experience. It is the wellspring of many forms of artistic expression. Creative work, by definition, demands the invention of multiple solutions to problems with whatever resources are available. The creative process is inherently spiritual, it is "about us, about the deep self, the composer in all of us, about originality, meaning not that which is all new, but that which is fully and originally ourselves" (Nachmanovitch 1990).

Improvisation in theatre, as in no other artistic endeavor except jazz, has particular purposes, distinctive functions. It serves as a tool and as a technique, as an approach to performance and production as well as a stand-alone theatrical genre. Improvisation can be traced historically from the earliest dramatic rituals to the initial telling of *The Odyssey,* on to sixteenth-century Commedia dell'Arte troupes (which used familiar plots and stock characters), through to stand-up comics and nightclub performers (who use situations and characters to entertain an audience—something with which users of this book need not concern themselves), Chicago's Second City, Broadway's *Godspell,* Joseph Chaikin's Open Theatre and the Group Theatre (which arrived at performance scripts through improvisation), and to the mid-1990s' Blue Man Group.

Despite the widespread use of improvisation, it was not until the publication of Caruso and Clemens' *The Actor's Book of Improvisation: Dramatic Situations for the Teacher and Actor* (1992) that there was a single, comprehensive source of material on which to base improvisations. That book, a thoughtfully crafted response to a long-standing need experienced by acting teachers and students in professional training and higher education arenas, is the template for *The Young Actor's Book of Improvisation.*

As its title suggests, this book is intended to respond to the same need for a single sourcebook, this time for students between the ages of seven and eleven, and for the teachers who work with them. In the author's notes for her play, *In a Room Somewhere,* playwright Suzan Zeder writes, "This play is aimed at the child within the adult and the adult within the child who exists in all of us" (Zeder 1988, vii). In that sense, this book is intended both for young people and adults. In formal, full-fledged productions, whenever possible, it is best to cast children as children and adults as adults. Author Sandra Caruso directed a most successful production of *The Prime of Miss Jean Brodie,* in which the roles of the faculty in the play were performed by school faculty, while the roles of the students were performed by student actors.

Many of the situations in this book are from plays successfully mounted, with casts of multiracial, multiethnic, able-bodied and physically challenged young people and adults. Many of the plays on which these situations were based have been produced at Boston's Wheelock Family Theatre, of which author Susan Kosoff is a founder and the producer. Wheelock enjoys a national reputation as a venue that produces multicultural and intergenerational theater. For example, in *Charlotte's Web,* the title role was played by an African American woman, while Wilbur was played by an Asian man; a Latina woman played the title role in *Peter Pan;* an Asian girl played Dorothy in *The Wizard of Oz;* and a Latino man played Sammy in *The Dark at the Top of the Stairs.* This casting practice is based on the premise that, in order for theater to be relevant in the 1990s, casts should reflect the diversity represented in the larger society. Equally significant is the way in which the understanding of a character, even the interpretation of a play, is enhanced, for actors and audience members alike, by challenging the traditional approach to casting.

Some of the situations in this book are included precisely because the characters are strictly defined by their race, age, sex, culture, or class. This allows actors to explore and to play characters who are like and different from themselves. For example, *Escape from Slavery: The Autobiography of Frederick Douglass,* provides several solo moments, because they allow all students, regardless of their race, the opportunity to experience the realities of a young boy's life as a slave. By contrast, some of the situations, such as *Swimmy* or *The Wind in the Willows,* are included because they are *not* specific about race, age, sex, culture, or class, thereby allowing students and teachers the opportunity to experience and appreciate the difference that casting choices can have on plays and players.

The Young Actor's Book of Improvisation addresses a broad age range of young people, from childhood to mid-adolescence. Many creative drama books are directed toward elementary-school-aged children. The difference in the intended audience reflects an inherent difference in purpose. In conventional informal drama, creative drama, and theater games, there is a strong emphasis on the creative process, with an explicit commitment to play for play's sake. The technique used in this book makes rigorous demands on students by structuring situations that require that they work in greater depth than is usually required by theater games. Although the focus remains on the actors' development as opposed to audience response, the technique helps them make the transition to the serious study of acting.

Young people—those who have completed several sessions of creative drama or, depending on their ages, have taken a few classes in the basic techniques of acting, as well as those who have begun scene-study work or performed in full productions—need the process outlined here to further their growth, for it is a developmentally appropriate next step. Improvisation is presented as a disciplined method for learning the craft of acting, as opposed to a laissez-faire activity.

Improvisation, as an acting technique, refers to the method actors use to create their own dialogue and actions in imaginary circumstances. These imaginary circumstances may be created by the actors themselves or may be provided by an acting coach or director. Using this technique, an actor surrenders to the excitement of not knowing what is coming next. One may know what *might* happen, but no one knows what will happen. Improvisation pushes people to become comfortable with surprise (Nachmanovitch 1990).

Many drama teachers, as well as theater directors, use improvisation as a tool to help actors make situations more immediate and more real for themselves. Sandra Caruso uses background improvisations extensively in her acting classes at UCLA to help students fill in their characters' lives. For example, if a scene is about a spouse asking for a divorce, students improvise the couple's first meeting, the marriage proposal, the birth of their first child, and the incidents that led to the failure of the marriage. Theater directors also use improvisation when actors, who have been rehearsing or performing a play for a long period, get stale and stop listening to each other. Improvisation can force them to listen again; they do not know what is coming next.

As Stephen Nachmanovitch noted in *Free Play:* "Martha Graham described this as 'a vitality, a life force, an energy, a quickening that is translated through you into action, and because there is only one of you in all time, this expression is unique. And if you block it, it will never exist through any other medium and will be lost'" (1990, 25).

We have given structure to these improvisations, because, as Nachmanovitch says, "structure ignites spontaneity" (1990). We have provided some form to keep the improvisations from wandering off course. Picasso confined his palette, in his "blue period," to the color blue, and this opened a whole new vista for him. Actors will ultimately be working in a tight structure dictated by lines, blocking, objects, sets, lights, and a director. These improvisations provide some boundaries in terms of the characters, place, background information, and situation. Within this external structure, the actors can play. Since everything is held together by structure, the imagination is free.

Successful exploration demands that there be some concrete element to focus and clarify what the actor is doing. Strasberg pointed out that,

> When you tell a pianist, "Improvise," he immediately asks, "What do you want me to improvise on?" He knows so many things he can do that he finds it difficult to limit himself to one thing. When you say, "Chopin," he then takes a phrase from Chopin and improvises. Improvisation is very difficult to do without a theme. There must be something given as a problem. (Strasberg 1965, 277)

Improvisation is used to achieve a deeper understanding of physical actions and conflict. Actors are active, not passive; they move from the external to the internal, from the physical—how characters reveal themselves through body movement and vocal expression—to the psychological— why characters behave as they do. Improvising the material before approaching the text motivates students to investigate the original source upon which the improvisation is based. Even reluctant readers will want to read the original source material, because they already have some familiarity with it or have the impetus to learn about it. On the other hand, improvising the material *after* approaching the text can enrich students' understanding.

Improvisation, as suggested for use here, is rooted in the method of "active analysis" developed by Stanislavski late in his life and still in use in Moscow's theater training studios. When the actors are rehearsing a play, they begin acting even before they know the words of the script. They are able to get to the heart of their work by using an improvisational approach. This approach is the cornerstone of this book.

James Thomas brings attention to Michael Chekhov's phrase, "the psychology of the improvising actor," as an apt description of the need for characters to come naturally from within. Chekhov believes that improvisation helps actors begin to think, feel, and even speak like their characters before they fully understand a text intellectually. As long as the process is not forced and is trusted to work, the right combination of actor and character eventually emerges. The actors need the words of the text and want to use them.

> Expressing the play in their own words, finding the essence of the play through physical action, developing the logic of the play to its correct conclusion—seems to make the play arrive

out of the imaginations of the actors themselves and not from memorization and repetition of the lines. The actors reach the kind of deep understanding of the text, improvisationally, that is often unsuccessfully tried in standard rehearsals using intellectual analysis alone. This is what Stanislavski meant when he said that characterization should emerge unconsciously from the actors. (Thomas 1993)

Young people are as open and as able to work in this manner as are adult actors.

This book provides a bridge from informal drama and theater games to formal drama using established text. Working with the structured improvisations found here will allow young people to approach an actual working text with increasing insight and sensitivity. When actors—of any age—are asked to create their own situations for improvisation, there is a tendency for the themes that are generated to be repeated with great regularity. By providing situations that are not defined by or limited to actors' personal experiences, they are challenged to expand the limits of their imagination; indeed, they come to understand that they can play any character in any situation.

These improvisations are divided into chapters by specific categories. Each category consists of a group of situations that allow particular acting problems to be addressed. This format is, to a large extent, a matter of organizational convenience; the categories are somewhat arbitrary. All of the situations in the book can be used to work on a number of acting problems outside the specific category to which they have been assigned. Furthermore, some elements of drama, such as relationships and subtext, are present in all situations, regardless of the designation assigned.

Many of the situations in *The Young Actor's Book of Improvisation* have been field-tested with young people between the ages of seven and eleven in regular and special education classrooms in school and theater settings, in order to identify weaknesses or problems in the material. The data gathered as a result of this research have been analyzed and included as comments, which accompany each improvisation. These comments are meant as guidelines for use by student and teacher. The intent is to enlarge what can happen in a scene rather than to limit or predetermine the outcome. For instance, young actors may laugh during situations that make them emotionally uncomfortable. Nervous laughter is not unusual when people hear shocking news, such as the death of a loved one. Let the laughter play itself out, as long as it is the truth of the moment. If the students are not ready to deal with the situation, let it go; they still will have had an acting experience. Further, the actors might imagine or remember a pet animal that has died, to make treading this territory feel less threatening.

Sometimes, the outcome of an improvisation will run contrary to the original source material. It is important to remember that even though the source for a given situation is either tragic or comic, the resulting improvisation does not need to fall into that category. The same scene can be acted successfully from different perspectives. In fact, it is an instructive and sometimes provocative process to approach the same material from different standpoints. It is in this same spirit that time periods, as well as the sex, age, race, culture, or class of a character, can be changed to add different dimensions to the scene, to inject humor, or to reflect reality.

The purpose of the background information provided for each improvisation is to increase the actors' understanding of the characters they are playing. It is not meant as exposition for the actors. Too much explanatory dialogue is deadly; it dissipates any real tension or excitement in a scene, causing the improvisation to seem artificial and lifeless. Teachers must help students guard against their inclination to talk too much, to explain too much, to "tell the story." When teachers find specific background information crucial to an understanding of a particular scene, it is best to give the information to the actors at the beginning of the improvisation.

The notion that "less is more" is often critical in acting. To illustrate this point, Caruso uses the example of an actor, playing a mother, who says to her daughter, "Your father and I have been divorced for twelve years and are planning a reunion." Logically, the daughter would know how long her parents have been divorced: the mother would not have to give her daughter this information. As a sign in Sanford Meisner's office read, "An ounce of behavior is worth a pound of words."

Finally, the effective use of this book requires that every situation be treated with respect by actor and coach. Students need to internalize and personalize the information provided. Teachers need to trust that it has been assimilated. Both must be willing to let the improvisation happen and to believe that the characters will develop in an organic process. Neither teacher nor student should assume the role of director but, rather, should allow the acting to be spontaneous, so that the process will lead to interesting terrains in sometimes unexpected territories.

It is our hope that *The Young Actor's Book of Improvisation* will challenge students and teachers to take risks, to try new ways of being and acting that will lead to an ever-increasing understanding of themselves and others, as well as of the world in which they live.

A User's Guide

Source: The original source—novel, short story, film, poem, play—from which the situation is taken. ("Film by" signifies that the film was directed and written by the same person.) There are many sources that have multiple situations. These situations are numbered chronologically in the index by source title.

Characters: The number and gender of the characters, their names, their relationship to each other, and miscellaneous identifying information. In many improvisations, the gender of the characters is not necessarily germane to the exercise; an improvisation for two males may, in some cases, be done by two females. (Occasionally, when a character's name is not considered intrinsic to the exercise, it is not given.)

Place: The specific locale in which the situation occurs. If relevant, the time period in which the scene takes place is also given.

Background: Story information necessary for the actors' understanding of their characters and the situation, leading to the point at which the improvisation is to begin. In some instances, there will be more than one improvisation from the same source, but they will be placed in different chapters. All such scenes are listed in the index. For further background information, actors are encouraged to read all improvisations from the same source.

Situation: Details of the specific situation on which the improvisation is based. This is where it all comes together.

Comments: Notes and tips to the actors and teachers—helpful hints, as well as warnings of possible pitfalls inherent in the material. This section often contains supplemental background information that may further enhance the actors' understanding of story and character.

Situations within chapters are organized alphabetically. A list at the start of each chapter classifies the situations according to number and gender in the following manner:

> one male, one female
>
> two females
>
> two males
>
> ensemble (any situation with more than two characters)

A number of the improvisations in this book have been supplied by students from Sandra Caruso's acting classes at the UCLA School of Theater, Film and Television. Teachers are encouraged to have their students write their own improvisations. In addition, for a complete listing of the sources used in the text, readers may refer to the bibliography at the back of this book.

1

Climactic Moment/ Discovery

Every scene is filled with realizations or insights that characters will discover for the first time. This chapter contains situations in which the characters make especially significant discoveries, which may be about themselves or the other characters. Discoveries about another character may be: he loves me, he hates me, he's lying to me, he's scared, and so on. Discoveries about oneself might be: I love him, I hate him, I'm scared, I'm in charge, and so on. Old or new secrets may be revealed. If the actor constantly makes new discoveries in these situations, the improvisations will never be dull, but will always be exciting. In *Audition*, Michael Shurtleff discusses that in the play, *Whose Afraid of Virginia Woolf*, the scenes between Martha and George "would be boring and tiresome if the actors did not find what is new, what is different, what is particularly at stake in the scene. Acting is a whole series of discoveries. . . . Ask yourself: What is new?" (1978, 58–59).

These realizations, or insights, are the "aha" moments in life; the very kind of discovery that is life-changing. Usually these heightened moments occur at the climax of a play, film, or novel, or at a climactic moment in a character's life. Although characters experience important changes throughout a dramatic work, it is the specific time at which these changes happen, or a realization occurs, that is considered a climactic moment.

1

CLIMACTIC MOMENT/DISCOVERY SITUATIONS

One male, one female
Aladdin and the Wonderful Lamp
Beauty and the Beast
Inside
Peter Pan

Two males
Hercules
Journey

Ensemble
Arthur and the Magic Sword
A Blue-Eyed Daisy
"El Dia Que Fuimos a Mirar la Nieve" (The Day We Went to See Snow)
Doors
Emil and the Detectives
The Emperor's New Clothes
The Great Gilly Hopkins
Journey to Topaz
The Miracle Worker
Pocahontas
Sarah, Plain and Tall
The Secret of Roan Inish
Something Is Missing
The Tinder-Box

Source: *Aladdin and the Wonderful Lamp,* a play by James Norris

Characters
One male, one female: Aladdin, a young boy of humble circumstances; Adora, a young girl, the daughter of the sultan

Place
The outskirts of a city in North Africa

Background
Aladdin has run away and is hiding behind a rock from his mother—a good woman who does not understand him. He sees a young girl, Adora,

running and looking about. When she hears a man's voice calling her, she stops and hides behind the rock, too. Adora has run away from her father to see the world and to find out what other boys and girls are like.

Situation
Aladdin and Adora discover each other while hiding behind the rock and introduce themselves. Although they come from different places—he from a tailor shop and she from the sultan's palace—they are both lonely and eager to experience the world. As they gallop off on pantomimed horses, they are attracted to each other's spirit of adventure.

Comments
The two young people are delighted to have met each other. The scene should be charged with energy and excitement.

Source: *Arthur and the Magic Sword,* a play by Keith M. Engar

Characters
Two male, one female: Arthur, in his early teens; Kay, in his early teens; Marion, a little younger

Place
The courtyard of a castle in Britain

Background
Merlin the magician took Arthur—King Pendragon's newborn son and heir to the throne—to live out of harm's way in the home of Sir Hector and Lady Lenore. There, Arthur grew up with Kay and Marion, believing that they were his siblings by birth and not knowing that he was destined to become the king of England.

Situation
Arthur and Kay have an archery contest, which, to everyone's surprise, Arthur wins. Kay is furious. To even the score, he tells Arthur that he is not Kay's real brother, and that his mother and father are not really his parents.

Comments
The actor playing Arthur should feel the shock of discovering that what he has always believed is not true. The actor playing Kay must decide how he feels about having delivered such startling news, while Marion, shaken by the announcement, feels great empathy for Arthur, whom she admires.

Source: *Beauty and the Beast*, a Walt Disney movie by Gary Trousdale and Kirk Wise, animation screenplay by Linda Woolverton

Characters
One female, one male: Belle, a young woman; the Beast

Place
The Beast's castle

Background
At first, Belle was the Beast's prisoner in his castle. Gradually, they became friends, with the Beast falling in love with Belle. When Belle's father fell ill, the Beast allowed her to go to him if she promised to return to the castle. Belle kept her promise and returned only to find Gaston, Belle's rejected suitor, and the Beast engaged in bloody combat high atop the castle roof. Gaston stabbed the Beast, took a misstep backward, and fell to his death on the cobblestones below. The Beast lay helpless on the roof.

Situation
Belle runs to the Beast, who is overjoyed to see her. She has come back to him after all. Crying, Belle falls to her knees to embrace him. Leaning down to kiss him, she tells the Beast that she loves him. Suddenly, the Beast is transformed into a human being—indeed, into a prince.

Comments
Belle and the Beast have come to love one another. He is overjoyed that she kept her promise and came back to him; he can now die without regret. Belle, upon seeing the wounded Beast, realizes that she loves him. It is their love that causes his transformation. Of course, in the film, they live happily ever after, but the actors must resolve the situation in a way that is real and believable. The challenge with such a familiar and romantic story is to keep the feelings rooted in reality.

Source: *A Blue-Eyed Daisy*, a novel by Cynthia Rylant

Characters
Five females: Ellie, age eleven; Eunice, Wanda, and Martha—her older sisters; Linda, their mother

Place
A hospital emergency room

Background

Okey, the girls' father, is a coal miner. He drinks too much and drives too fast in his Chevy pickup truck. Although Okey seems invincible, his family has always worried that his reckless behavior will result in a serious accident.

Situation

What they had long feared has happened, and the family has been called to the hospital. Linda goes in to see Okey. She returns to the waiting room, very upset. Okey is not dead, but he is unconscious and fighting for his life. Ellie begs her mother to let her see Okey, but Linda refuses.

Comments

Each person will react differently in this situation. They all have unfinished business with their father. The actors must establish their relationships with each other. The girls spend the night in the waiting room not knowing whether their father will live or die. In the morning they find out that he will survive. If the actors choose, they might also enact this part of the situation.

See index for other improvisations from this source.

Source: "El Dia Que Fuimos a Mirar la Nieve" (The Day We Went to See Snow), a short story by Alfredo Villanueva-Collado, translated by Cynthia L. Ventura, in *Where Angels Glide at Dawn: New Stories From Latin America*, edited by Lori M. Carlson and Cynthia L. Ventura

Characters

Ensemble: Any number of boys, girls, and adults

Place

A park in San Juan, Puerto Rico; noontime, 1952

Background

In 1952, Felisa Rincon de Tautier, mayor of San Juan, brought snow in an airplane from the United States to the children of Puerto Rico.

Situation

The children come to the park to see this strange substance on the ground. The snow is beginning to melt in the hot sun, and the children abandon themselves to a thorough exploration of this amazing phenomenon, staring, touching, smelling, and playing. They have no idea what snow is; it is completely new to them.

Comments

This is a sense memory exercise in the exploration of the snow. If the actors have experienced snow before, they should try to remember their first encounter with it. Others may never have seen real snow and will need to imagine what the substance is like. Before the improvisation begins, the teacher may ask what the students know about snow. Answers will vary, of course, according to the part of the country in which they live. In the story, snow is seen through the eyes of one child who did not find it so thrilling. Through this exercise, youngsters will discover for themselves what this experience would be like.

Source: *Doors,* a play by Suzan L. Zeder

Characters

Two males, one female: Jeff, eleven years old; Ben, his father; Helen, his mother; Sandy, Jeff's friend (optional)

Place

Ben and Helen's bedroom

Background

For a long time, Jeff has overheard his parents having terrible arguments behind their bedroom door. He turns up the TV so as not to hear them. Also, Jeff is aware that his father leaves every night and comes home for breakfast. His parents have never told him that anything is wrong.

Situation

One day, after an especially loud argument, Jeff opens the door to his parents' bedroom and sees his father, Ben, packing a suitcase. Jeff asks him what he is doing. Ben says that he and Jeff's mother are splitting up. Soon Helen enters and, for the first time, the three of them face the reality of the situation. Jeff tries very hard to keep his parents together.

Comments

This play is based on a true story. The "door" is significant; this is the first time that the symbolic door has been opened to allow these three people to face each other. It is important for the actors playing the parents to know the specific nature of their marital problems. In the play, Jeff is unable to keep his parents together (the father leaves), but let this improvisation develop its own ending. The actors may unconsciously bring in elements from their own lives, which is fine.

Also, the actors can improvise a preliminary scene between Jeff and his friend, Sandy, in which Jeff talks about his parents and asks for her help. Students may tap into personal experiences in this situation.

Source: *Emil and the Detectives,* a play by Erich Kaestner, adapted and translated into English by Cyrus Brooke

Characters
Three males, two females: Emil Titchburn, a young boy; an asthmatic gentleman; a man in a bowler hat; Mrs. Jacob; a thin woman

Place
A compartment in a passenger train en route to London

Background
Young Emil is traveling to London to visit his grandmother and his cousin, Polly. His mother pinned money to the inside of his breast pocket for safekeeping; she was terribly worried that he would be robbed. Also in the train compartment are Mrs. Jacobs, who talks too much; a thin woman, who sneezes frequently and crochets constantly; an old gentleman with asthma, who wheezes and reads his newspaper; and a man in a bowler hat.

Situation
Each of the adults establishes a relationship of one sort or another with Emil as the train rattles along the tracks toward London. As each traveler disembarks from the train, the man in the bowler hat moves in closer to Emil until the two of them are alone in the compartment. When Emil falls asleep, the man steals his money and exits.

Comments
Each of the actors plays a role in establishing the story, especially the bowler-hatted thief. However, the focus of the situation is on Emil's moment of discovering that his mother's worst fear has come true—he has been robbed.

Source: *The Emperor's New Clothes,* a musical by Ruth Perry (book), Allan Jay Friedman (music), and Paul Francis Webster (lyrics), based on the story by Hans Christian Andersen

Characters
One female, three males, ensemble: Vicki, daughter of the royal laundress, ten years old; the Prince of Transylvania; Dudley, his servant; the Emperor of Libertania; various court figures (optional)—the empress, stewards, guards

Place
The kingdom of Libertania

Background
All the weavers in the kingdom were on strike for better working conditions. When the prince and Dudley, who were just passing through, were falsely arrested as spies, they presented themselves as weavers able and willing to cut and fit and sew a new suit for the emperor's birthday celebration in just three days' time. They told all the people of the royal court that their weavings have magical properties. Whoever cannot see their woven cloth is not competent to do his job.

Situation
It is the occasion of the king's birthday celebration. Ladies and gentlemen of the court are all present, moving about and conversing. Also, the prince and Dudley are present. Ten-year-old Vicki has managed to find a spot from which to observe the festivities. Excitement mounts as people await the arrival of the emperor; they are nervous that they will be barred from all future court functions if they can't see the royal garments. Finally, the emperor enters, wearing a crown and carrying his scepter, strutting as if in full regalia. In fact, he wears only a pair of shorts and an undershirt. Everyone goes along with the masquerade, except for Vicki, who cannot help pointing out the obvious.

Comments
Each of the actors must come to terms with their own duplicity as they react to the truth spoken by the actor playing Vicki. The actor playing the emperor must decide whether to accept or deny the truth, and then he must decide to deal with Vicki and the others accordingly.

Source: *The Great Gilly Hopkins,* a novel by Katherine Paterson

Characters
Ensemble; Three females, one male: Gilly Hopkins, an eleven-year-old girl; Mrs. Trotter, her foster mother; a policewoman; William Ernest, Gilly's foster brother

Place
The waiting room of a bus station

Background
Gilly last saw her mother eight years ago. Since then, Gilly has gone from one foster home to the next. Her current foster mother, Mrs. Trotter, an

enormously heavy woman with a good heart, is devoted to being a good Christian. William Ernest, another foster child, lives in the house as well; he is mentally disabled. Mrs. Trotter cares for an elderly blind man, Mr. Randolph, who lives next door.

Gilly is treated very kindly by Mrs. Trotter, but all Gilly wants to do is find her real mother. A postcard from her mother arrived one day, with a return address in San Francisco. The message was one sentence long and gave no indication that her mother wanted her back. Nonetheless, Gilly stole one hundred dollars from Mrs. Trotter's purse and thirty-five dollars from the bookcase in Mr. Randolph's house for traveling money. Gilly went to the bus station and purchased a one-way ticket to San Francisco. Seeing that Gilly was only a child, the ticket seller called the police. The police notified Mrs. Trotter.

Situation
Mrs. Trotter and William Ernest have come to the bus station to bring Gilly home. A policewoman asks Mrs. Trotter if she wants to bring charges against Gilly for stealing money, but Mrs. Trotter does not. She asks Gilly if she wants to go home. Gilly says that home is with her mother in San Francisco. Since Gilly is reluctant to go with Mrs. Trotter, the policewoman suggests that they keep her at the police station overnight. Mrs. Trotter pleads with Gilly. William Ernest starts to cry, begging Gilly to come home with them. Finally, Gilly agrees to go.

Comments
Gilly has never been loved before, and this display of affection is foreign to her. She cannot believe that these two "weird" people love her. However, from their behavior at the bus station, it appears that they do. After Gilly returns to Mrs. Trotter's house, she begins to become attached to this strange group and, in fact, ends up taking care of them when they're ill.

A note to the actor playing Gilly: although Gilly comes to realize that these people actually care about her, her change in attitude is gradual. She doesn't instantly become a different girl at the bus station.

See also the following improvisation.

Source: *The Great Gilly Hopkins,* a novel by Katherine Paterson

Characters
Ensemble; Four females: Gilly Hopkins, an eleven-year-old girl; her grandmother; Courtney, Gilly's mother; Mrs. Trotter, Gilly's foster mother

Place
Three locations: the arrivals area at an airport; a telephone booth at the airport; and a telephone in the home of Mrs. Trotter

Background
Gilly last saw her mother eight years ago. Lately, Gilly has been living in a foster home with Mrs. Trotter and William Ernest, a mentally-disabled boy. Gilly has grown to love Mrs. Trotter and William, but now Gilly has been legally placed with her grandmother. The most important thing in Gilly's life is to be reunited with her mother. Today, her mother is arriving from San Francisco for a visit, and Gilly is very excited. She believes that her mother has come to take her home forever. Gilly and her grandmother await the plane's arrival.

Situation
Gilly has waited almost her whole life for this moment. The plane lands. Her mother, Courtney, is the last passenger to deplane. Gilly has been looking at the same picture of her mother for years and was expecting a much younger and prettier woman. Courtney wastes no time in making it clear that she came only because her airfare was paid for and that she plans to stay no more than three days. Then, Courtney and her mother (Gilly's grandmother), who have not seen each other for eight years, begin to quarrel. Gilly is profoundly disappointed; her mother has no plans to take Gilly back with her.

Part two: Gilly calls Mrs. Trotter from a telephone booth at the airport. She begs Mrs. Trotter to let her come back. Gilly can't relate to her old-fashioned grandmother, and Gilly now knows that her mother doesn't want her. Gilly has grown to love Mrs. Trotter; she is more a mother to Gilly than anyone in the young girl's life. Mrs. Trotter, though she loves and misses Gilly, explains that Gilly must remain with her grandmother.

Comments
It is important for the actor playing Gilly to have great expectations of her mother. Gilly has been waiting eight years for this reunion, fantasizing that, once she is with her mother, life will be great and she will be happy. Her mother's indifference is devastating.

The actor playing Courtney must find believable reasons for her behavior. What, for instance, might be the actor's relationship with her *own* mother? Why has Courtney been away from home for eight years? How does she feel about Gilly?

The actor playing the grandmother must also delve into her relationship with her daughter. Why does she think Courtney has been away for so long? Is she somehow responsible?

Mrs. Trotter is undoubtedly tempted to ask Gilly to come back. However, she realizes that Gilly cannot return; furthermore, she doesn't want Gilly's grandmother to suffer in loneliness.

After the telephone call, which Gilly makes in secret, she returns to face her grandmother, her mother—and reality. A reconciliation is one possible resolution to this scene.

See also the preceding improvisation.

Source: *Hercules,* a Walt Disney movie directed by Ron Clements and John Musker, screenplay by Ron Clements, John Musker, Bob Shaw, John McEnery, and Irene Mecchi, story by Barry Johnson

Characters
Two males: Hercules, as a young boy; Zeus, his father, a mythical god

Place
The temple of Zeus

Background
Hercules, the son of Zeus and Hera, was kidnapped by the Fates, Pain and Panic, under strict orders from the god of the underworld, named Hades. The Fates took Hercules to earth, where he was to be murdered. Although he managed to escape death, Hercules could not return home to Mount Olympus, because he had become mortal. He was adopted by a kind couple, who loved him dearly, but Hercules just never fit in. He was unable to control his amazing strength. Eventually, Hercules decided to try to find a place where he belonged. His parents gave him a farewell memento: the gold medallion with a symbol of the gods that he had been wearing when they found him.

Situation
Hercules begins his search at the temple of Zeus. He kneels before the giant statue of Zeus to pray for guidance. The statue of Zeus comes to life! Hercules learns that Zeus is his father and that he cannot return to Olympus until he proves himself a true hero on earth.

Comments
The actor playing Zeus, who is all powerful, must feel—and show—the strain of being unable to help his own son return home. The actor playing Hercules must go through many changes during this interaction—fear, shock, joy, determination. The resolution of the situation must come naturally out of the dialogue between father and son.

Source: *Inside,* a UCLA student film by Mario Hernandez Jr.

Characters
One male, one female: Pepe, nine years old; his teacher

Place
An elementary school classroom

Background
Pepe is very close to his brother, who has just been put back in jail for parole violations. Lately, Pepe has been the butt of a number of practical jokes at school. A classmate handed him a drawing of a woman with one big breast. The teacher found the drawing on Pepe's desk, assumed that he had drawn it, and sent him home from school. Pepe did not want to squeal on his classmate, so he took the blame. Then, when he got home, Pepe's father beat him. The next day, the same classmate took a video game out of the teacher's desk and slipped it into Pepe's school bag. The teacher discovered that the game was missing and questioned her students. When the game was found in Pepe's bag, he was sent home once again and, once again, his father beat him.

Situation
Pepe discovers that his father has a gun. Pepe loads the gun, puts it in his school bag, and takes it to school. During class, he takes the gun from his bag and points it at the teacher. She asks him to let the children leave the room, and he does. The teacher is left facing Pepe and the loaded gun in Pepe's hand.

Comments
In the actual incident on which the film is based, Pepe turns the gun on himself. The actors can let the ending develop naturally. (Maybe the teacher can talk Pepe out of it.) They must assume that the gun is loaded.

This is a sad story. Obviously, no one at school knew what was brewing in Pepe's mind. He was sensitive to the students' ridicule, the humiliation of being sent home and punished for things he had never done. Even if he had done these things, they were small offenses that did not require the strict punishment he received from both his teacher and his father.

Recognize that Pepe's actions were not prompted by vengeful anger. Rather, he felt very alone and very hopeless. His father loved him, but did not know how else to behave with him. His mother was unable to protect him. His teacher was not very perceptive. Pepe's only ally, his brother, was in prison. Overwhelmed, nine-year-old Pepe felt that he had to deal with the whole world all by himself.

Source: *Journey,* a novel by Patricia MacLachlan

Characters
Two males: Journey, an eleven-year-old boy; his grandfather

Place
Grandfather's house

Background
One day, Journey's mother packed her bag and went away, leaving Journey and his sister to live with their grandparents. Grandfather said that Journey's mother would never return, but Journey didn't believe him.

Situation
Journey wants to look at the old family photographs—happy pictures of Journey and his sister as babies, with their mother and father—so he pleads with Grandfather to let him see them. Grandfather insists that there aren't really that many. When Journey continues to pester him, Grandfather confesses that Journey's mother tore them up.

Comments
Journey is angry with his grandfather for saying that his mother won't come back. The boy is looking for clues that will help him understand why his mother left. He thinks that the photographs will help him to find the answer. Deep down inside he somehow believes that, by seeing the pictures of their once happy family, he'll be able to resurrect it. Grandfather knows what Journey is trying to do, and it is painful for him to have to reveal that the pictures have been torn up.

See index for other improvisations from this source.

Source: *Journey to Topaz,* a novel by Yoshiko Uchida

Characters
Ensemble; Two females, five males: Yuki Sakane, eleven years old; Mrs. Sakane; Mr. Sakane; Ken Sakane, Yuki's brother, eighteen years old; three non-Japanese FBI men

Place
The home of the Sakane family in Berkeley, California; December, 1942

Background
This is an autobiographical account by an eleven-year-old girl, Yuki. When war broke out between the United States and Japan in December 1941, Japanese people became "enemy aliens." A month after the bombing of Pearl Harbor, President Franklin D. Roosevelt issued an executive order concerning areas from which Japanese people could be excluded. Persons of Japanese ancestry were uprooted from their homes on the West Coast and transported to internment camps. The majority were citizens of the United States, including Yuki's family.

Situation
One day, three men from the FBI appear at the Sakane's house. They say that they have orders to apprehend men who work for Japanese firms in the area and that Mr. Sakane is to come with them immediately. He is not even allowed to change from his gardening clothes to more formal attire. The rest of the family must prepare to evacuate their home and report to a church designated as the civil control station for all Japanese people.

Comments
The Sakanes are a dignified, law-abiding, middle-class family living in a suburb of Berkeley. Actors playing the Sakanes need only imagine that *they* are suddenly ordered to evacuate their homes because they are a certain color or because they live in a particular city. The Sakanes are shocked and confused, but they must obey the FBI. (In the book, Mr. Sakane is removed a few weeks before the rest of the family is ordered to evacuate. For the sake of the improvisation, these two actions have been combined.) The family may bring only those belongings that they can carry by hand. The packing can be incorporated into the improvisation.

It is important to appreciate the formality of the Sakanes' cultural traditions. Mrs. Sakane, for example, still wears a hat and gloves when she goes out, even to the market. She is very concerned that the house be left clean for whoever moves in when they leave. And they have beloved neighbors, to whom they must bid farewell.

See also improvisations from the following sources: *Journey to Topaz* and *Journey Home*.

Source: *The Miracle Worker,* a play by William Gibson

Characters
Ensemble; Three females, one male: Helen Keller, eleven years old; Annie Sullivan, Helen's teacher; Kate Keller, Helen's mother; Captain Keller, Helen's father

Place
A pump in the front yard of the Kellers' house in Tuscumbia, Alabama; the 1880s

Background
After a bout with measles, Helen Keller became blind, deaf, and mute. Her parents, at their wits' end, hired Annie Sullivan, a teacher from the Perkins Institute for the Blind in Boston, to work with Helen. Helen is an undisciplined and unruly child. The Kellers are sorry for her and cater to her every whim, and she has become very spoiled, throwing tantrums when she doesn't get what she wants.

Shortly after her arrival, Annie Sullivan requested that she and the uncontrollable Helen be locked up together in the summer house. Captain Keller reluctantly consented, but gave Annie just two weeks. Annie then battled it out with Helen, who kicked, spit, and hurled objects at her. Annie persisted, knowing that teaching Helen obedience and language were the keys to releasing her from darkness.

Situation
The two weeks are up. A homecoming dinner has been prepared for Helen, with all her favorite foods. Helen has learned to fold her napkin and to eat with utensils; until now, she only ate with her hands. However, back with her parents, Helen rebelliously refuses to use a napkin or utensils and continually throws them on the floor, with Annie putting them back in Helen's hands each time.

Finally, Annie grabs Helen and takes her outside. They go to the pump; Annie pumps out some water. She continually spells words with her fingers into the palm of Helen's hand, hoping that Helen will attach the word to the object. So far, Helen has not made the connection. Suddenly, and for the first time, Helen realizes that when Annie spells *water* with her fingers, it is the name of the liquid that is coming out of the pump. She says, "Wa Wa." Annie yells to the Kellers, exclaiming that Helen "knows." Annie, with her fingers, spells *mother, papa,* and *teacher,* each time placing Helen's hands on the individual, so that she can make the connection between the word and the person. Helen Keller has now learned that everything has a name.

Comments

This is an extraordinary moment for Annie, Helen, the Kellers—and the world. Until this day, Helen's soul had been buried deep within her; through Annie, she was she able to find her humanity. Helen finds consciousness through language. She had related to Annie as her enemy until now because Annie would not cater to her tantrums. It has been almost a life-and-death struggle between the two.

This moment also has great significance for Annie; she had been orphaned and nearly blind as a child. She educated herself while undergoing multiple operations to improve her vision. She was also haunted by her inability to protect her little brother, who died in the institution in which they lived. Teaching Helen is Annie's "resurrection."

Source: *Peter Pan,* a novel by James M. Barrie

Characters

One male, one female: Peter Pan, a boy who will never grow up; Tinkerbell, a fairy

Place

Never Land

Background

Captain Hook and his pirates captured Peter's friends—Wendy, John, and Michael Darling, and the Lost Boys—while Peter was sleeping. Hook found the passage to Peter's hideaway and crept inside. He added five drops of poison to medicine that Wendy had left for Peter, then skulked away.

Situation

Tinkerbell wakes Peter to tell him that the pirates have captured Wendy and the boys. Peter leaps up, ready to run to their rescue. But before he leaves he remembers his promise to Wendy. Despite Tinkerbell's warnings, Peter intends to drink his medicine. Tinkerbell is devoted to Peter; she grabs it away from Peter and drinks the poisoned medicine. Once he realizes what she has done, Peter is distraught. Tinkerbell tells him that she will not die if children believe in fairies. Peter appeals to the world of children (in the case of the play, to the audience) to say that they believe and to show it by clapping their hands. Slowly and steadily, Tinkerbell returns to life. The scene climaxes with Peter running off to save Wendy and the boys.

Comments

In the play, Tinkerbell the fairy is represented by a flash of light no bigger than a fist, and speaks in a tinkle of bells. Here, an actor can play the role of Tinkerbell or the actor playing Peter can simply imagine her and represent her part by his actions and reactions. The actors should focus on the life and death urgency of this scene—first as Tinkerbell tries to prevent Peter from taking his medicine; then as Peter desperately tries to save Tinkerbell's life.

See index for other improvisations from this source.

Source: *Pocahontas,* a Walt Disney movie by Mike Gabriel and Eric Goldberg, written by Carl Binder, Susannah Grant, and Philip LaZebnik

Characters

Ensemble; One female, two males: Pocahontas, a young American Indian girl; Chief Powhatan, her father; Captain John Smith, an Englishman

Place

Virginia Colony; the seventeenth century, sunrise

Background

A group of Englishmen, led by Governor John Ratcliffe, sailed to the part of the New World where Pocahontas lived. It was John Smith's responsibility to make sure that the Indians didn't interfere with the English as they built their settlement. Quite by accident, Smith and Pocahontas, Chief Powhatan's favorite daughter, met and fell in love. When Kocoum, the man Powhatan intended Pocahontas to marry, discovered Smith and Pocahontas kissing, he attacked Smith. Thomas, Smith's friend, stumbling upon the scene, shot and killed Kocoum.

Situation

Smith, mistakenly accused of the murder of Kocoum, has been condemned by Chief Powhatan to die at sunrise. Smith rests his face against a large stone slab. Powhatan raises his club to execute Smith, when Pocahontas appears out of nowhere and throws herself over Smith's body.

Comments

The actor playing Powhatan must decide how he will react to Pocahontas. He feels totally justified in what he is about to do, but must allow himself to be challenged by his daughter's actions. Pocahontas's objective is clear—to save Smith's life—but the actor playing her must figure out how to persuade her father to see things her way. Smith will experience the range of emotions one would feel as one faces the real possibility of death. Using words would be to no avail; Smith speaks English and the American Indians do not.

Source: *Sarah, Plain and Tall*, a novel by Patricia MacLachlan

Characters
Ensemble; Two males, two females: Papa; Caleb; Anna, Caleb's younger sister; Sarah

Place
A train station in the midwest; the nineteenth century

Background
Caleb and Anna's mother died the day after Caleb was born. The children are lonely and want a mother. Papa, who used to sing every day when Mama was alive, has stopped singing. He placed an ad in the newspaper for a wife and received an answer from a woman named Sarah, who lives in Maine.

Situation
Sarah arrives at the train station, where Papa and the children are waiting to meet her. Caleb and Anna have many questions for Sarah; there are so many things they want from her.

Comments
It will take time for a good relationship to develop in this family. The arrangement may work or it may not. Sarah loved the ocean in Maine; the flat land of the midwest, far from the sea, makes her unhappy. There is a lot at stake here for all involved. If the actors have read the book, they should forget how it turns out; at this moment, nobody knows what will happen. The actors should think about questions they might ask a strange woman who they hope will be their mother.

Source: *The Secret of Roan Inish*, a film by John Sayles based on the novel *The Secret of Roan Inish* by Rosalie K. Fry

Characters
Ensemble; One male, two females: Grandfather; Grandmother; Fiona, their ten-year-old granddaughter

Place
The grandparents' home in Ireland

Background
Fiona's family once lived on the island of Roan Inish, but poverty and loneliness drove them back to the mainland three years ago. During the move, Fiona's infant brother, Jamie, floated out to sea in his cradle and was given up for dead.

Fiona and her grandfather returned to Roan Inish on a fishing expedition. Exploring the abandoned dwellings, Fiona found signs that someone was living there. She encountered a naked, three-year-old boy— her brother Jamie. He fled, terrified, never having seen another human being before.

Situation
Fiona tells her grandparents that she glimpsed her brother, Jamie, on the island. At first, they don't believe her; it seems impossible that a baby could have survived for three years, alone, on a deserted island. Besides, Fiona is ten years old, with a head full of fantasies. There is an added element: a storm is brewing. It would be dangerous to take the boat to the island to search for Jamie at this time.

Comments
The grandparents have grieved over the loss of their grandson, and the terrifying moment when the child drifted off to sea must be stamped forever in their minds. Fiona's story is unbelievable, but they desperately want to believe it.

See index for other improvisations from this source.

Source: *Something Is Missing,* a play by Jane Staab

Characters
Ensemble; One male, one female, one male or female: Benjamin, a young teen-ager; Lisa, his younger sister; a squirrel

Place
The backyard of a house in a small town

Background
Benjamin used to be happy and fun-loving, playing with his younger siblings, but he suddenly seemed to lose his joie de vivre. All he did was mope about. To Lisa, it seemed that happiness had left him, so she went

off to search for happiness for her brother. After facing many challenges, she discovered, with help from a hermit-like creature of the forest and a squirrel that had been following her, that happiness comes from within. The hermit gave Lisa a beautiful flute for her to take to Benjamin.

Situation
Lisa arrives home with great expectations of the flute and anxious to share what she has learned. However, Benjamin appears as downcast as ever, even when Lisa gives him the flute. She leaves Benjamin alone. The squirrel, which has continued to follow Lisa, picks up the flute as if to run away with it in order to get Benjamin's attention. He sees the squirrel and moves to retrieve the flute. In doing so, he looks at it more carefully, then decides to play it.

Comments
The progression of Benjamin's emotions go from complete emptiness to curiosity about what will happen when he tries the flute to his sensations upon discovering that he can create music. The child playing Benjamin does not have to be able to play the flute nor, for that matter, is an actual flute necessary for the situation. Although a recorder is probably the best substitute, the playing of the flute can be mimed. Remember: what is important is Benjamin's reaction to making music.

Source: *The Tinder-Box,* a play by Nicholas Stuart Gray

Characters
Ensemble; One male, three males or females: Peter, a young soldier; three dogs

Place
A garret in the town of Kastleburg; the sixteenth century

Background
Peter hurt his arm in battle and is no longer needed as a soldier. Today, he met an old woman (a witch) who asked him to climb down a hollow tree to fetch her tinder-box for her—and a great fortune for himself. The items were guarded by three dogs, but Peter succeeded in disarming the sentries by befriending them. Upon his return, the old woman was so rude to Peter that he became flustered and gave her his own tinder-box rather than the one he had taken from the tree. Because of her unpleasant treatment, he refused the treasure. That night, he found himself in a dark, dank garret in the Flying Horse Inn, cold and hungry.

Situation

Peter uses the old woman's tinder-box to light a candle. When he strikes the flint once, there is a great flash and the black dog from the hollow tree appears. The dog leaves momentarily and returns with a bag of copper coins for Peter. With the black dog's help, Peter begins to realize that the tinder-box is magic: if he strikes it twice, the black dog and a white dog will appear, and if he strikes it three times, the white dog will appear. Furthermore, each will bring bags of silver and gold coins if they are asked. Slowly, Peter comes to realize that immense good fortune has come to him.

Comments

The actors playing the dogs may or may not use words to communicate with Peter, but they need to show their devotion to him as well as the magic properties of the tinder-box. Peter begins to see the many opportunities that will now be his, and he is grateful to the dogs.

2

Confrontation/ Conflict

If drama, by definition, is about conflict, then acting is about confrontation. Although there may be subtle differences between the two, they usually go together hand in glove. Both conflict and confrontation make exciting theater. Actors must learn to paint their characters into a corner, to stack the deck so that characters are thrust into inevitable confrontation with one another. In other words, conflict consists of wanting something from someone that he or she won't or can't give. In these situations, actors must work hard to make their needs strongly felt and to attain their objectives.

Actors often assume that to create conflict they must instigate a heated argument. However, as Lee Strasberg said, "The actors can do the whole scene without a single word. You could sit for half an hour just making little sounds and noises and could still build up the whole sense of the conflict between you and him" (the actors) (Strasberg 1965, 277). The situations in this chapter have been selected to help actors learn to face conflicts from which they cannot escape. They need to rely on their intuition and improvising spirit—as opposed to their logic and dialogue.

CONFRONTATION/CONFLICT SITUATIONS

One male, one female
Charlotte's Web
Fly Away Home
Freckle Juice
Mirette on the High Wire
Protecting Marie

Two males
"The Boy Who Painted Christ Black"
Shiloh

Ensemble
Abiyoyo
The Arkansaw Bear
The Great Gilly Hopkins
Meet Felicity
"Ooka and Two Honest Men"
Shiloh
The Travels of Babar
The Woman Who Outshone the Sun

Source: *Abiyoyo,* a South African folktale as told by Pete Seeger (improvisation written by Maggie Nolan Donovan)

Characters
Two males, one male or female, ensemble: A father; his son; Abiyoyo, a giant; townspeople (optional)

Place
A village in South Africa; long ago

Background
Once there was a father and a son who lived in a small South African village. The father had magical powers and could make things disappear with a wave of his wand. He was always playing tricks on people. His son had a ukulele, on which he plinked and plunked, morning and night, from one end of the village to the other. At last, the people ordered this annoying pair to pack up their wand and ukulele and leave.
　　One morning soon after, the villagers awoke and felt the earth shaking, and they saw a huge shadow blocking out the rays of the sun. They realized at once that it was Abiyoyo, a terrible giant who often came to terrorize the people. "Run for your lives!" they cried, but the father took up his magical wand, the son grabbed his ukulele, and they went forth to meet Abiyoyo.

Situation
The father plans to make Abiyoyo disappear, but first the son must get him to lie down. The son sings a song all about Abiyoyo, which delights

the giant. In great glee, he dances heavily, around and around, until his head spins with dizziness and he falls to the ground.

Comments
Abiyoyo is both scary and silly. His gigantic size and bad temper make him very dangerous, but his vanity causes him to succumb to the song. Father and son work as a team. The actor playing the giant can have fun trying to feel his body as huge.

Source: *The Arkansaw Bear,* a play by Aurand Harris

Characters
Ensemble; One female, three males or females: Tish, a young girl; a mime; the World's Greatest Dancing Bear; the Great Ringmaster

Place
The woods in Arkansas

Background
Tish just learned that her grandfather, whom she adores, is about to die. She ran off to her favorite tree and wished on the first star to understand why this terrible thing had to happen. A mime, who never speaks, and the World's Greatest Dancing Bear, appeared at Tish's tree.

Situation
The bear, worried, is in a hurry and out of breath. He is running away from the Great Ringmaster—death. The three begin to establish a relationship, just as the Ringmaster arrives. The bear, who is not ready to die, tries to escape his fate. The others try to help him. Tish bargains with the Great Ringmaster for more time.

Comments
Tish, the bear, and the mime are desperate in their efforts to buy time for the bear. They have yet to make peace with the concept of death. The Great Ringmaster is friendly and pleasant, but authoritative; he knows that death comes to everyone. No matter what the bargain they make now, it will only delay the inevitable.

Source: "The Boy Who Painted Christ Black," a short story by John Henrik Clarke

Characters
Two males: Mr. Duval, a school principal; Erin, a ten-year-old student

Place
Mr. Duval's office in an elementary school for black children in Georgia; 1948

Background
Every year the school district sponsors a state pride art contest. In the past, the "colored" schools were not allowed to enter. But now that Mr. Duval is running such a successful school, the white superintendent of schools has allowed Mr. Duval's students to enter the contest. Erin, one of the students, painted a beautiful picture of a black Christ. Erin's teacher proudly presented the painting to Mr. Duval, saying that it would be a perfect entry for the state pride art contest. The superintendent saw the painting in Mr. Duval's office and was horrified. He demanded that Mr. Duval dispose of it immediately.

Situation
Erin comes to see Mr. Duval, excited that his picture has been entered in the contest. Mr. Duval must tell Erin that his picture will not be shown.

Comments
The actor playing Mr. Duval should decide what he tells Erin. How do you explain to a ten-year-old boy why Christ can't be black—when Erin and Mr. Duval are, themselves, black? Christ, in fact, may well have been black. It is a great disappointment to Erin, who felt so proud of his accomplishment—and it *is* a good painting. Mr. Duval is in a precarious position; he knows he will lose his job if this picture is entered in the contest.

Source: *Charlotte's Web,* a novel by E.B. White

Characters
One male, one female: Mr. Arable; Fern Arable, his young daughter

Place
The Arable farm

Background
Fern saw her father with an ax and asked her mother what he was doing. Mrs. Arable told her daughter that one of the baby pigs that was born the night before is a runt, and Mr. Arable was about to kill it with the ax. Fern was horrified that this pig was to be killed just because of its puny size.

Situation
Fern rushes to her father, who is en route to kill the runt of the litter. She wants to stop him from killing the pig. He believes he knows best and that

he is doing the right thing; the runt will probably die, anyway. But Fern is completely committed to saving the pig's life.

Comments
To a large extent, the conflict here is between reason and emotion. Eventually, Fern wins. Her emotional reaction is so strong that it touches her father, a kind, loving man who believes that killing the pig is the reasonable thing to do.

See index for other improvisations from this source.

Source: *Fly Away Home,* a film by Carroll Ballard based on Bill Lishman's autobiography, screenplay by Robert Rodat and Vince McKewin

Characters
One female, one male: Amy, twelve years old; Amy's father

Place
The kitchen in their home in rural Canada

Background
Amy discovered an abandoned goose nest and has been hiding the eggs in her room. Now they have hatched, and the kitchen is filled with baby geese—and their droppings.

Situation
Amy's father tells her that she may not keep the baby geese; they are destroying the house. He can't even eat on the kitchen table because it is covered with geese; everything is filthy and unsanitary. He wants the geese put outside. Amy pleads that they'll catch cold outside, so they must stay in the house for now.

Comments
Amy has recently lost her mother and empathizes with these orphaned baby geese. They are the glue that is holding her together at the moment; if they are taken away from her, she will probably fall apart. This improvisation would work well with the solo moment, when Amy discovers the abandoned nest.

Another good situation in this story revolves around an animal control officer's visit to Amy's home. The officer wants to clip the geese's wings, which would mean that they will never be able to fly. The officer's argument is that the geese could not survive if they flew away because they have not learned yet how to fend for themselves. However, Amy and her father don't agree. They want the geese to have their freedom, and they put up quite a fight to save the baby geese.

The outcome of this story is quite thrilling. The geese "imprinted" with Amy and followed her everywhere. When they matured, they had to be taught how to migrate south. Amy's father invented a flying machine that looked like a very large mechanical goose. He taught Amy to operate it so that the geese would fly along with her. She showed them a route south along which they could find water. Word of Amy's expedition spread, and people all along the route cheered her on as she flew by. The geese reached their destination, and, in fact, they return to Amy and her father every year.

See index for other improvisations from this source. For other situations concerning a child's relationship with a pet, see improvisations from the following sources: *Protecting Marie, Shiloh, The Biggest Bear,* "A Boy and His Dog," and "The Chicks.".

Source: *Freckle Juice,* a novel by Judy Blume

Characters
One male, one female: Andrew Markus, nine years old; Sharon, nine years old

Place
An elementary school classroom

Background
Andrew sits behind Nicky Lane at school. Nicky has an abundance of freckles, which Andrew envies greatly. Sharon, a classmate, gave Andrew a recipe for freckles—an awful mixture of things his mother would have on hand in the pantry. Andrew went home from school to make the concoction. His mother was playing cards at a neighbor's house, so he had the kitchen all to himself. He concocted and drank the mixture. The results were most unpleasant. And, of course, there were no freckles.

Situation
After having been sick all night, Andrew goes to school the next day and sees Sharon. How does he deal with her?

Comments
The actors can decide on the ingredients Sharon prescribes. What might Andrew say to Sharon when he sees her? In the story, he paints freckles

on his face. It could be fun to see Sharon's reaction—she might think that, by some miracle, her prescription had worked.

Source: *The Great Gilly Hopkins,* a novel by Katherine Paterson

Characters
Ensemble; Three females: Gilly Hopkins, an eleven-year-old girl; Gilly's grandmother; Mrs. Trotter, Gilly's foster mother

Place
Mrs. Trotter's home

Background
Gilly has not seen her mother, Courtney, for eight years. Gilly is presently living in a foster home with Mrs. Trotter and William Ernest, a mentally-disabled child. Initially, Gilly hated the place. All her previous foster families had rejected her; it was only a matter of time before this family would too. She wrote to her mother, complaining that Mrs. Trotter was a religious fanatic and William Ernest was retarded, that she had to take care of everyone and so had no time to do her schoolwork.

In the meantime, Gilly tried to run away to find Courtney in San Francisco. When Mrs. Trotter was called to retrieve the runaway from the bus terminal, she and William Ernest cried and cried, begging Gilly to come home. This expression of emotion finally convinced Gilly that Mrs. Trotter and William Ernest really did love her. Since then, Gilly has loved them back and taken care of them. Gilly has finally found a home.

Situation
One day soon after the episode at the bus station, a woman comes to Mrs. Trotter's door and announces that she is Gilly's grandmother. Courtney had received Gilly's letter and called her mother to rescue Gilly from this supposedly abusive home. A social worker made all the arrangements, and the grandmother has come to take Gilly to live with her. By this time, Gilly has come to love her foster home and doesn't want to leave. Besides, she wanted her *mother* to rescue her, not her grandmother.

Comments
The actor playing Gilly must realize that she has painted herself into a corner: Gilly did write the letter, and there is no way to reverse that fact. She got a reaction, but not the one she wanted. And since Gilly is still only eleven years old, she is under the authority of the courts and has no

choice. Her grandmother is a total stranger to her—an old-fashioned woman to whom Gilly cannot relate. The grandmother thinks she is doing something kind; in reality, she is lonely and needs Gilly more than Gilly needs her. The grandmother expected to be greeted with open arms, but this is not the welcome she gets. Gilly puts up a fight to stay with Mrs. Trotter, who has now become her surrogate mother, but Mrs. Trotter does not have the legal power to keep her. Watching Gilly leave is heartrending for her.

See index for other improvisations from this source.

Source: *Meet Felicity*, a novel by Valerie Tripp

Characters
Ensemble; One female, two males: Felicity Merriman, nine years old; Mr. Merriman, Felicity's father; Jiggy Nye, a disreputable fellow

Place
Williamsburg, Virginia; the eighteenth century

Background
Felicity's curiosity was piqued when she heard that Jiggy Nye had won a horse on a bet. She went to meet the horse, which was still wild. She fell in love with the animal and named her Penny. Jiggy said that anyone who was able to ride the horse could keep her. When Felicity learned that Jiggy was beating and starving the poor horse into submission, she made secretive daily visits to the stable, taming and feeding the grateful steed.

Situation
Felicity rides Penny home to show her father how well the horse responded to gentle treatment. As Mr. Merriman begins to tell her that she must return the horse to its rightful owner, Jiggy Nye appears. He accuses Felicity of stealing and demands that she return his property.

Comments
The objectives for all three actors are straightforward. The actor playing Felicity must show her great affection for the horse and her indignation at the injustice the horse suffers at the hands of Jiggy. Jiggy's typical mean-spiritedness has been accelerated to righteous fury: someone has stolen his

horse. And Mr. Merriman has deep ambivalence; he understands his daughter's behavior, but he cannot condone it.

Source: *Mirette on the High Wire,* a story by Elizabeth Arnold McCully (improvisation written by Maggie Nolan Donovan)

Characters
One female, one male: Mirette, a young girl; the Great Bellini, a middle-aged man

Place
A small room in a boarding house in Paris, France; the late 1800s

Background
Mirette's widowed mother runs a boarding house for actors, musicians, and other performers who are passing through Paris. Lately, a mysterious stranger has taken up residence. When he arrived, he requested a private room at the back of the house and said that he would take his meals alone in his room.

One day Mirette looked out into the courtyard and saw the stranger walking along the clothesline. Fascinated, she begged him to teach her how to walk the tightrope. He refused. So Mirette taught herself. After much practice, she succeeded in walking the clothesline from one end to the other. The stranger watched, amazed and impressed and, at last, agreed to become her tutor. They worked together every day, and, as Mirette's skill increased, the rope was raised a little higher.

A new arrival at the boarding house recognized the stranger as the Great Bellini, a world-famous tightrope walker who once fried an egg while balanced on a high wire stretched across Niagara Falls! However, Bellini had lost his nerve—and circus wisdom says that once you lose your nerve it's gone forever.

Situation
When Mirette hears the story, she rushes to Bellini's room. She demands to know if the story is true. He acknowledges his identity and admits his fear. Mirette begs him to try to overcome it so that he can return to the life his fear forced him to abandon. Bellini does not want to disappoint the little girl, but his terror consumes him.

Comments
Mirette has fallen in love with the high wire; her feet will never be as happy on the ground again. Her discovery of the truth about Bellini fills

her with disappointment and outrage. She feels betrayed. Bellini is torn between his devotion to Mirette and his fear. At the end of the story, but not as a direct result of this confrontation, Mirette and Bellini meet in the middle of a high wire strung over the rooftops of Paris.

See index for other improvisations from this source.

Source: "Ooka and Two Honest Men," a story in *Japanese Folktale Stories About Judge Ooka,* collected by Venceslava Hrdlickovà and Zdenek Hrdlicka

Characters
Three males or three females: Saburobei, a master carver; Chojoro, a noodle man; Judge Ooka, a wise man

Place
Japan; a long time ago

Background
Saburobei was very poor, but he did the best he could to support his wife and children by carving figurines. One day, a rich merchant bought one of Saburobei's most elegant statuettes for three gold pieces! Saburobei was delighted. He could now pay off all his debts before the new year. As he hurried home, he dropped the bag of money that he was so eager to show his wife. Chojoro, a noodle man passing from house to house, noticed a white packet on the ground. In it, he found the gold coins and realized that he could use them to pay off all his debts before the new year! Then he saw a note in the packet identifying it as Saburobei's, who Chojoro knows is a poor man with a family to support. Chojoro must decide whether to keep the money or to return it.

Situation
Chojoro decides to return the money to Saburobei. However, Saburobei won't take the money back; he believes in fate and thinks that bad luck would come his way should he accept the return of the money. Chojoro found it, so it belongs to him. Chojoro insists that Saburobei take the money back. The two men decide to take their dilemma to wise Judge Ooka, who will settle the matter for them.

Comments
The actors should understand that the power of fate was very real to the characters. Saburobei truly believes it would be bad luck to take his own

money back. Chojoro wants to be an honest man and to feel good about his deed. The actor playing Judge Ooka can solve the problem in any way he wants. The resolutions of these Japanese tales are clever and strangely logical.

See also improvisation from the following source: "A Debt Repaid."

Source: *Protecting Marie,* a novel by Kevin Henkes

Characters
One female, one male: Fanny Swann, a twelve-year-old girl; Henry Swann, her father

Place
Their home near Boston, Massachusetts

Background
Fanny's father, Henry, is an artist, and he is going through a mid-life crisis. He came home on Christmas Eve, left a note saying that he couldn't face the family party, and disappeared for the night. The Swanns had to open their presents without him.

Fanny had wanted a dog all of her life. She has a large collection of pictures of dogs, but she had given up hope that she would ever have a dog of her own. One day, several months ago, Henry was in a good mood because a prestigious gallery wanted to handle his paintings. So, he brought home a puppy for Fanny. She named it Nellie.

Nellie sneaked up to Henry's studio and had an accident on his Oriental rug. She chewed the legs of antique furniture, slept on the couch, cried at night, growled and nipped at Henry, and tore up the garden.

Situation
Henry tells Fanny that he can't paint anymore because the dog is driving him crazy. Fanny thinks that she'll die if he takes Nellie away, but he insists that she give up the dog. He asks her to write the ad for the newspaper. She also has to make a pile of Nellie's belongings and put them at the front door.

Comments
Putting Nellie's belongings at the front door can be done as a solo moment for Fanny; that happens sometime after the scene with her father. In the novel, Fanny's mother, Ellen, tries to explain how Henry feels. When the ad is answered, Fanny watches a man and woman drive off with her beloved dog. Fanny says that this is the worst thing that has ever

happened to her. These scenes can be used to extend this improvisation, or they can be done as a solo moment for Fanny.

Many actors can relate to the strong feelings that Fanny has for Nellie and how terrible it feels to give up a dog you love. Remember that Henry is not unfeeling or deliberately cruel. He simply must do his work. He had no idea how difficult it would be to have a puppy around the house.

For other situations concerning a child's relationship with a pet, see improvisations from the following sources: *Shiloh, The Biggest Bear,* "A Boy and His Dog," "The Chicks," and *Fly Away Home.*

Source: *Shiloh,* a novel by Phyllis Reynolds Naylor

Characters
Ensemble; Two males, one female: Marty Preston, an eleven-year-old boy; Mr. Preston, his father; Mrs. Preston, his mother

Place
Marty's home in the hills near Friendly, West Virginia

Background
One day, as Marty was passing the old Shiloh schoolhouse, he came upon a young beagle. He learned that the dog belonged to Judd Travers, a neighbor who mistreats animals. Once, Marty saw a dog in the woods with a bullet through its head, and he suspects that Travers was responsible.

Marty's father made him return the dog to Travers. Marty had named the dog Shiloh, but Travers refused to call it by name; he doesn't bother to name his dogs. When Shiloh saw Travers, the beagle cowered. The next time Travers took the dogs hunting for rabbits, Shiloh ran away again, looking for Marty.

Situation
Marty is determined not to return Shiloh to Travers. He confronts his parents, but they tell Marty that there just isn't the money to feed the dog and take him to the vet. Besides, keeping Shiloh would be as good as stealing. Travers paid money for that dog, and he will never give him up. But, Marty loves Shiloh and would do anything for him.

Comments
The character of Judd Travers must be seen clearly by the other characters. There is no doubt that he is mistreating his dogs. He is a tough customer; if he found out that Marty had his dog, he would cause a lot of trouble. The important thing for Marty is his devotion to Shiloh. His parents are

not unfeeling, but they have a hard-enough time putting food on their table every night as it is. They cannot allow Marty to keep the dog.

See also the following improvisation. For other situations concerning a child's relationship with a pet, see improvisations from the following sources: *Protecting Marie, The Biggest Bear,* "A Boy and His Dog," "The Chicks," and *Fly Away Home.*

Source: *Shiloh,* a novel by Phyllis Reynolds Naylor

Characters
Two males: Marty Preston, eleven years old; Judd Travers, a middle-aged man

Place
Outside Judd Travers' house in Friendly, West Virginia

Background
Marty found a stray dog, which he named Shiloh. It turned out that Shiloh belonged to a neighbor, Judd Travers, who mistreats his animals. Marty begged his parents to let him keep Shiloh, but they refused on the grounds that it would be stealing. Reluctantly, Marty returned Shiloh to Travers, but, at the next opportunity, Shiloh ran away and came back to Marty. Again, Marty's parents told him to return the dog to Travers, but Marty has been keeping Shiloh secretly penned up and sharing his own meals with the dog.
One night, another dog attacked Shiloh and wounded him severely. Marty's father discovered the injured Shiloh and took him to a veterinarian. Travers found out that Marty had his dog and demanded it be returned as soon as it was healed. Today Marty must return Shiloh to Travers.
Marty knows that this is his problem and that he must face it alone. He also knows that Travers has a gun and might even shoot him, but he loves Shiloh too much to part with him without a fight. Marty goes early in the morning to tell Travers that he will not return the dog. On his way through the woods to Travers' house, he sees Judd shoot a beautiful doe. Deer are out of season, and there is a sizable fine for poaching.

Situation
Marty accosts Travers, who is startled to see him. Marty, aware that he has the upper hand, threatens to report Travers to the game warden. There is blood on the snow as evidence. But Travers doesn't feel threatened by an eleven-year-old boy; he doesn't believe Marty would turn him in. But Marty doesn't give up easily. The two finally come to an agreement— which the actors can discover for themselves.

Comments
To the actor playing Judd Travers: Don't dismiss him as an animal abuser; understand this man's tortured personality. He is very lonely; he has no love in his life. Marty's feelings for Shiloh are incomprehensible to Travers. His ownership of this dog is important for his ego, and he drives a hard bargain. Marty, on the other hand, finds a strength within himself that surprises Travers.

See also the preceding improvisation.

Source: *The Travels of Babar,* a children's story by Jean de Brunhoff, translated from the French by Merle Haas

Characters
Ensemble; One male, one female, ensemble: Babar, the young king of the elephants; Queen Céleste, his wife; several fierce and savage cannibals

Place
A remote island

Background
Newlyweds Babar and Céleste decided to take their honeymoon trip in a hot air balloon. At first they enjoyed smooth sailing. Then, they were caught in a terrible storm and blown out to sea. A twist of fate sent the balloon crashing and collapsing onto an island, leaving the two marooned in the middle of nowhere.

Situation
Babar and Céleste leave the balloon with their belongings to find shelter. After setting up camp and eating breakfast, Babar goes off to explore the island while Céleste naps. Several inhabitants of the island—cannibals— discover Céleste sleeping and tie her up. They are celebrating her capture when Babar returns.

Comments
The cannibals are terrified by the elephants' massive strength. Babar and Céleste—royalty through and through—are indignant at the audacity of the cannibals. Although the situation is physical in nature, it need not be violent. In fact, a direction for the scene may very well be to have fun with the confrontation.

Source: *The Woman Who Outshone the Sun,* a story by Rosalma Zubizarreta, Harriet Rohmer, and David Schecter, from a poem by Alejandro Cruz Martinez (improvisation written by Maggie Nolan Donovan)

Characters
Ensemble; One female, three males or females, ensemble: Lucia Zenteno, a beautiful woman; a river; two children; townspeople (optional)

Place
The entrance to a cave outside a small town in Mexico; long ago

Background
One day, a beautiful woman arrived in a small village in Mexico. Her name was Lucia Zenteno, and her past was shrouded in mystery. She was pleasant, but kept to herself. Some people said her beauty outshone the sun.

Each day, Lucia Zenteno bathed in the river. Soon, the river fell in love with her. It rose up and flowed through her hair, with all its fish and otters. When Lucia finished bathing, she would comb the river out of her hair. The elders advised the people to treat Lucia with honor and respect; she understood the ways of nature. But, she was so different from them that the people were afraid. They began to treat her so cruelly that at last they drove her from the village.

When Lucia went to say good-bye to the river, it refused to leave her. The river went away with Lucia and a terrible drought came upon the land. Weeks passed, and the people grew more and more desperate. Finally, they went in search of Lucia. They found her in a cave.

Situation
Lucia is standing at the entrance of the cave with the river in her hair. When the townspeople approach, she turns her back on them. Two children step forward to ask for forgiveness and to beg for the river's return.

Comments
Lucia, clearly a goddess, feels compassion for the people. However, she was deeply wounded by their treatment of her and wants to teach them to be more loving.

3

Fantasy

People spend a great part of their lives fantasizing—imagining themselves living in another time or place or becoming other people. For the actor in particular it is beneficial to move away from the naturalistic world and into the realm of make-believe. The actor's task is to experience and identify with make-believe situations as though they are real. Michael Chekhov wrote, "The imagination of an actor is not that of an ordinary person. I want to know how to do things which I am not able to do" (1985, 41).

Stanislavski once suggested to a student that he imagine himself to be a tree. Just saying that you are a tree doesn't make you believe it. You have to ask yourself certain questions, such as: If I were a tree, what would I do? Where am I? What are my surroundings? How do they affect me? What do I hear? What do I see? What is my purpose? What are the surrounding circumstances that would move me emotionally or incite me to action? Once the actor has definite visual images, he is living the fantasy. In Stanislavski's words: "Every movement you make on the stage, every word you speak, is the result of the right life of your imagination" (1936, 67).

The situations in this chapter allow actors to create a world that does not exist, that is pure fantasy. In *Lessons for the Professional Actor*, Michael Chekhov suggests that there are three stages in exercising the imagination: the first is to imagine things we already know; the second is to imagine things we've never seen but have heard about; and the third is to imagine things that do not exist. Even though the actor is inventing elements that never have been or, perhaps, never can be, sometimes the most fantastical things prove to be true, such as the existence of life on other planets. Human beings possess the ability to see things that do not exist, to create mental pictures. The actor's ability to create a mental picture is essential, and these improvisations should be a stimulus. The characters are real, feeling human beings in fantastical situations. After attempting these improvisations, actors will return to more realistic circumstances with a fresh, perhaps more inventive, perspective. Stanislavski said "imagination plays by far the greatest part." In his book, *An Actor Prepares,* Stanislavski makes reference to a drawing of a set design, planned for the last act of a Chekhov play about an expedition to the arctic. It was painted by a man who had never left the suburbs of Moscow; he painted from his imagination. Stanislavski then points out sketches for a play about life on other planets. In this case, the artist is relying on fantasy.

FANTASY SITUATIONS

One male, one female
The Frog Prince Continued

The Mischief Makers

Nightingale

"The Other Frog Prince"

Peter Pan

A Por Quinly Christmas

"The Princess of the Sea"

"La Rebelion de los Conejos Magicos" (The Rebellion of the Magical Rabbits)

Stuart Little

The Tale of Jemima Puddle Duck

The Tale of the Shining Princess

Tuck Everlasting

Two females
"The Answer Backer Cure"

The Russian Cinderella

Two males
Coon Cons Coyote

Fish Is Fish

The Tale of Peter Rabbit

Ensemble
Alice's Adventures in Wonderland

The Bear's Advice

"Beautiful Brown Eyes"
The Blue Bird
Cinderella in China
"Doc Rabbit, Bruh Fox, and Tar Baby"
Frederick
In a Room Somewhere
Katy No-Pocket
"The Lion, Bruh Bear, and Bruh Rabbit"
The Lion, the Witch, and the Wardrobe
"The Mer-Woman out of the Sea"
The Mischief Makers
Mr. Popper's Penguins
The Native American Cinderella
Pippi Longstocking
The Rat and the Lion
Swimmy
The Tale of the Shining Princess
Tuck Everlasting
Two Foolish Goats and a Monkey
The Velveteen Rabbit
Where the Wild Things Are
Winnie-the-Pooh
The Wizard of Oz

Source: *Alice's Adventures in Wonderland,* a novel by Lewis Carroll

Characters
One female, three males or females: Alice, a young girl; the March Hare; the Hatter; the Dormouse

Place
The home of the March Hare in Wonderland

Background
Alice arrived in Wonderland by following a rabbit down a hole. She has wandered all over, had many adventures and met a variety of zany and amazing creatures.

Situation

Alice arrives at the home of the March Hare, where she finds the Hare and the Hatter sitting at a table having tea, with the Dormouse fast asleep between them. All three are quite mad. Alice joins them, uninvited, for a mad tea party. They tell riddles and stories, sing songs, and carry on in a variety of absurd ways until their rude behavior finally causes Alice to leave in disgust.

Comments

The actors playing the March Hare and the Hatter, with a little help from the Dormouse, must be as outrageous as they can be. The actor playing Alice must try to make sense of a nonsensical situation.

See index for other improvisations from this source.

Source: "The Answer Backer Cure," an extract from the book *Mrs. Piggle-Wiggle* by Betty MacDonald

Characters

Two females: Mary O'Toole, a young girl; Penelope Parrot, a parrot

Place

Mary's bedroom

Background

Mrs. Piggle-Wiggle is very small, smells like cookies, and has a lump of magic on her back. She lives in an upside-down house. All the children in town adore her. And, since Mrs. Piggle-Wiggle has the magical power to cure children of bad behavior, all the grown-ups love her too.

Mary O'Toole has been terribly rude lately, answering back to her teacher and to her parents. Aghast at her daughter's impudence, Mrs. O'Toole called Mrs. Piggle-Wiggle for help. Mrs. Piggle-Wiggle's cure arrived in the shape of Penelope Parrot.

Situation

Mary comes home from school and is delighted to find the parrot. It's not long before Mary discovers, to her dismay, that she and Penelope have something in common: a nasty answer to everything.

Comments

At first, Mary finds the parrot funny. Slowly, though, she begins to understand the effects of rude behavior.

See index for other improvisations from this source.

Source: ***The Bear's Advice,*** **a fable as told by Nigerian storyteller Ndubisi Nwafor Ejelimna to Sandra Caruso (1996)**

Characters
Ensemble; Three males or females: Ije; Uche; a bear

Place
Two locations in Nigeria: Ije's house in a village and a narrow pathway in the bush

Background
Ije and Uche are friends who do many things together. Ije is slim and Uche is fat. Ije invited Uche to accompany him on a weekend visit to his grandmother's house in another village about four miles away. Uche, however, was afraid of the wild beasts that infest the thick forest between the two villages. Ije told him that they will both be well armed; he, Ije, will bring his gun, while Uche will bring his bow and arrows. They will stand together and defend themselves in the event of any attack. Uche finally agreed and they left for the trip.

Situation
Ije and Uche are in the middle of the forest when a bear appears in the distance. Ije runs away as fast as he can and climbs up a tree. Uche, being fat, cannot run very fast, and the bear almost catches him. Uche remembers that his father once told him that bears do not eat dead animals. So, he pretends to drop dead. The bear rushes up to him and sniffs him, snuffling all around Uche's face and ears to see whether or not he is dead. Uche remains very stiff. The bear is disappointed and goes back into the forest.

Ije then climbs out of his tree and runs back to where Uche is still lying on the ground, frozen with fear. Ije tells him that the bear has gone away, and Uche rises. Ije says that he saw the bear putting his mouth and nose in Uche's face and ears. He asks Uche if the bear said anything to him. Uche says that the bear gave him some very useful advice: never go with a friend who runs away from you when you are in trouble.

Comments
This is a fable and therefore has a moral: the bear's message is sound advice to be kept in mind when choosing friends. A friend in need is a friend indeed.

Source: "Beautiful Brown Eyes," a story in *African-American Folktales for Young Readers*, collected and edited by Richard and Judy Dockrey Young

Characters
Ensemble; Two females, two males: A beautiful young girl; her mother; her father; her younger brother

Place
Along the Oueme River in Benin, on the Atlantic coast of Equatorial Africa

Background
In the season when the girl with beautiful brown eyes became old enough to marry, a great drought fell upon the land. Every day she went to the river bank to fill her jar with muddy water, until the day came when there was no more water.

The girl was crying bitterly, when a fish appeared to her and said, "Give me your jar and I will fill it for you." He put his mouth over the jar and spewed cool, clear water into it.

The girl returned for water day after day. On the seventh day, she kissed the fish and became his bride. The parents sent one of her younger brothers to see where the girl was getting the water. The boy saw his sister kissing the fish, and he ran home to tell the family this amazing piece of news.

Situation
The girl's family confronts her about marrying a fish. How can they explain this to their friends? Why was there no wedding?

Comments
This situation must be completely believable to the actors. The girl loves the fish, but her family is ashamed of this relationship. In-laws often express disapproval of a spouse. The situation may turn out to be humorous or tragic.

Source: *The Blue Bird*, a play by Maurice Maeterlinck

Characters
Ensemble; Two females; two males: Tyltyl; Mytyl, his sister; Mother; Father

Place
The children's bedroom in a woodcutter's cottage; Christmas

Background

Tyltyl has a pet blackbird, but he wishes it was a bluebird. When he and Mytyl fell asleep on Christmas Eve, a fairy appeared to them, saying that they must capture a special bluebird, one that doesn't change color in the daylight. She explained to them that she needs the bird for a little girl who is ill.

So, Tyltyl and Mytyl went on a journey in search of the bird. They traveled to the land of Memory where they visited their dead grandparents and found a bluebird, which was like a "blue glass marble." Tyltyl put the bird in a cage to take home, but when the bird was removed from the land of Memory it turned black.

They then went to the land of Future, where the bluebird turned pink. In the Palace of Night, the real Blue Bird—the only one that can live in the light of day—was hidden among many other bluebirds. Night, disguised as an old woman, begged the children not to open the door to the Palace of Night, but they opened it anyway. Thousands of birds were inside, but they all fell dead when struck by the rays of light. It appears that either the Blue Bird does not exist or it changes color when it is caged. In any event, the children could not catch it. They had to go home without it.

Situation

Mytyl and Tyltyl are sound asleep in their beds, just as they were before the arrival of the fairy. Their mother comes in to wake them up. Tyltyl and Mytyl are surprised to be home, and they are most happy and relieved to see their mother. They tell her about their journey, but she doesn't understand what they are talking about. While the children believe that they have been away from home for a whole year, their mother insists that they haven't left the room. Mytyl and Tyltyl describe the visit with their dead grandparents and all the other things that happened to them. Their worried mother calls in their father; she thinks the children may be ill. The parents also are worried that the children may have found the key to the brandy cupboard; they test the children to see if they are drunk.

Tyltyl and Mytyl look at Tyltyl's caged blackbird and realize that it's—blue! It is the very bird for which they were looking so long and so far away. It was here all the time.

Comments

This play is similar to *Our Town* and *The Wizard of Oz,* in that characters return after a long, strange journey and appreciate home more than they did before. The task for the actors is to create, with total believability, the idea that they have been away for a year and that they did see all these things. They must use their imaginations regarding the search for the Blue Bird. They can incorporate some elements from the background given here, but they can also invent; it's their journey. The parents, of course, are worried, because the children refuse to deviate from their story.

In the play, Tyltyl later gives his bird to a little girl next door, who is ill. Before his journey, he would never have parted with it. The gift of the bird makes the little girl well. The actors may decide to incorporate this into their improvisation.

See index for other improvisations from this source.

Source: *Cinderella in China,* a play by Lowell Swortzell in *Cinderella, The World's Favorite Fairy Tale*

Characters
Ensemble; Four females: Pear Blossom, a young girl; her stepmother; her two stepsisters

Place
A small house in China

Background
Pear Blossom did all the chores around the house. Her stepmother and two stepsisters were preparing for the royal procession. They called her Pigling, although she begged them to address her by her beautiful name, Pear Blossom. She believed that, if she completed all her households tasks, she would be allowed to attend the procession.

Situation
Pear Blossom is helping her stepsisters and her stepmother get into their dresses—tying their sashes and fastening their gowns. She announces that she has finished her chores and would like permission to attend the royal procession with them. At first, they tell her that this is a ridiculous request; then, teasing, they say that she may go—but only after she has husked all the rice and weeded the whole garden. Pear Blossom realizes that she can't do that much work in one day, so she won't be able to attend the procession.

Comments
This is a Cinderella story, so, of course, it has a happy ending. The animals Pear Blossom tends, the doves and a friendly cow, help her with her tasks so that she gets to watch the royal procession. Lin Yun, a rich young man, is visiting and looking for a wife. Guess whom he chooses?

However, the actor playing Pear Blossom has no idea that this happy ending is in store for her, and she is profoundly disappointed not to be allowed to attend the royal procession. Pear Blossom lives a very drab life, and this is the most exciting event to come to this village; to miss it would be awful.

In traditional Chinese theater, these plays are performed on a bare stage. They were originally performed by male actors only. The actors use a lot of pantomime and improvised scenes to guide the audience in the story.

See also improvisations from the following sources: *The Native American Cinderella, The Russian Cinderella,* and *The Rough-Face Girl.*

Source: *Coon Cons Coyote,* a play by Hanay Geiogamah, based on a Nez Perce tribal legend poem

Characters
Two males: Coyote; Birdboy

Place
A forest

Background
Birdboy is half bird, half boy; he claims to be the mightiest hunter in the forest. He steals attributes from all the other birds to enhance his own beauty.

Coyote is powerful and foolish, and he loves to play with his eyes. He also is always hungry, so hungry that one day he ate his younger brother, Coon. Coyote moved into a stone house to be protected from his enemies. Nobody could get in, but he couldn't get out. Since he was hungry, and his eyes were handy, he ate them. Then he had no eyes. A voice told him to use flowers in their place, but to be sure to get rid of the flowers before they wilted at sunset.

Situation
Birdboy is out hunting in the forest. Coyote encourages him to shoot a pheasant, which is sitting in a nearby tree. But Birdboy doesn't see any such pheasant. Coyote insists it is there. He taunts Birdboy, saying that he is not such a great hunter if he can't see it. He tempts Birdboy with the notion of the beautiful feathers that he could steal if only he can find the bird. Coyote says that he can see it because he has flowers for eyes. Birdboy wants to know where he can get some. Coyote offers to trade eyes, and they do. When the sun begins to set, Birdboy suddenly can't see. Furious at Coyote for his trickery, he chases after Coyote, who runs away laughing.

Comments

The actors have to go with the nature both of this story and these characters. Coyote should be persuasive enough to get Birdboy to switch eyes; Birdboy wouldn't give them up so easily. Nevertheless, his intense desire to be the greatest hunter and to shoot the most beautiful bird is Birdboy's downfall.

　　　To complete the legend: later on, some hummingbirds recognize Birdboy's eyes and snatch them away from Coyote. Eventually, Birdboy's eyes become little toys for his three granddaughters who also live in the forest.

Source: "Doc Rabbit, Bruh Fox, and Tar Baby," a folktale told by Virginia Hamilton, in *The People Could Fly*

Characters

Ensemble; Three males or females: Doc Rabbit; Bruh Fox; Tar Baby

Place

Near a brook and a briar patch in the forest

Background

Doc Rabbit drank an entire crock of cream that Bruh Fox had stored in the brook to keep cool. When Bruh Fox discovered what had happened, he wanted to take revenge on Doc Rabbit. So, he fashioned a little baby out of tar and left it for Doc Rabbit to discover.

Situation

Doc Rabbit comes upon Tar Baby and greets it politely. When Tar Baby is unresponsive, Doc Rabbit kicks it with one foot, which gets stuck in the sticky tar. When Tar Baby ignores his request to let him loose, Doc Rabbit kicks it with his other foot. Soon, Doc Rabbit manages to get all four feet and his head glued to Tar Baby. Bruh Fox returns to find Doc Rabbit entangled with Tar Baby and threatens to throw him into a fire. But Doc Rabbit slyly expresses his delight at the prospect, so Bruh Fox says he'll throw the rabbit into the briar patch instead. At this prospect, Doc Rabbit protests mightily (and falsely). Bruh Fox believes he has found the perfect punishment—he tosses the rabbit into the briar patch. Doc Rabbit, of course, is delighted—rabbits make their homes in such places.

Comments

Tar Baby can be played by an actor or imagined, although it is easier to physicalize getting stuck if an actual body represents Tar Baby. Young actors love being in on the joke in this improvisation. The situation allows them to play the characters in big, broad strokes, which fits well with the tale.

See index for other improvisations from this source.

Source: *Fish Is Fish,* a story by Leo Lionni

Characters
Two males or females: A frog; a fish

Place
A pond at the edge of the woods

Background
A minnow and a tadpole were inseparable friends. As time passed, they began to grow and change. One day the tadpole—now a frog—went off to explore the world, leaving the minnow—now a fish—behind in the pond. When at long last the frog returned, he told the fish about all that he had seen—birds and cows and people.

Situation
The fish is simply enthralled with these images of birds, cows, and people. He decides that he must see them for himself. He jumps out of the pond and onto the land, where he is unable to breath or to move. Fortunately, the frog is nearby and manages to push the fish back into the water. As the fish slowly revives, at home and safe in his own beautiful world, he acknowledges the truth of what the frog had told him long ago: "Fish is fish."

Comments
There are several ideas in this story that are worth keeping in mind:

1. two creatures that start out as identical infants can develop very differently and distinctively from one another;
2. despite the differences between the two, they can remain good friends; and
3. as a fish is meant to be in water, so we all do best in our own element.

Source: *Frederick,* a story by Leo Lionni

Characters
Ensemble; Five males or females: A family of field mice

Place
A stone wall in a meadow, close to an abandoned barn and granary

Background
All the mice, except Frederick, had begun to work day and night to gather and store food for the long winter ahead. They reproached Frederick for his indolence, but he explained that he is working too—gathering sunrays, colors, and words to fortify them against the winter.

Situation
Winter has come. The mice have been living comfortably in the stone wall with plenty to eat, telling stories, and having fun. But, when they eat up all the food and feel the cold of winter, they are miserable. Remembering Frederick's work and his supplies, they turn to him for help.

Comments
Frederick is a dreamer, a poet who shows the other mice the value of imagination and dreams in the face of dire circumstances. It is what he says about sunrays and colors and how he says it that comforts the other mice. Frederick's work and his supplies are truly appreciated. The actor can invent poetry.

Source: *The Frog Prince Continued,* a story by Jon Scieszka

Characters
One male, one female: the frog prince; his princess

Place
The living room of their castle

Background
The frog said to the princess, "If you kiss me, I'll turn into a prince," which she does and he does and they live happily ever after. But . . .

Situation
The frog prince and the princess have been married for several years, and the princess can't stand the prince's persistent frog-like behavior. He jumps around, does strange things with his tongue, makes awful noises. She tells him that his behavior will have to change. But the frog prince has his own problems. He's very unhappy being a prince; he would rather be a frog.

Comments

The actors can decide which frog behavior the frog prince exhibits. Think of everything a frog does. Remember: this is personification; he is not literally a frog. The actor playing the princess should have reached the point where she can't stand the prince's behavior anymore. The characters can find their own resolution. The prince yearns to be a frog, but what can he do? He's a frog living a man's life.

Source: *In a Room Somewhere,* a play by Suzan L. Zeder

Characters

Ensemble; Three males, two females: Cat; Mason; Kurt; Michael; Dudleigh. (The number of characters can vary.)

Place

A room somewhere

Background

Kurt was coaching his kid's basketball team; Mason was up on the roof just about to nail down a shingle; Michael was practicing the piano for the most important piano competition of his life two hours away; Dudleigh was taking her final exam at law school; while Cat remains enigmatic.

Situation

Suddenly, inexplicably, these people find themselves in the same room. They arrive, one at a time, in various ways. (Cat is already in the room at the beginning.) There isn't a door, window, or ceiling. All of these characters were in the midst of important activities in their lives when they were thrust into this unknown place. Eventually, one object from each person's childhood appears from out of nowhere.

Comments

The actors do not need to stick to the preliminary activities suggested above; they can choose to be doing whatever they like before they were catapulted into this space. Beforehand, each actor should think of a meaningful object from his childhood and, if possible, use it in the improvisation. This is an open-ended situation; the actors should furnish their own personal metaphors for, and concepts of, these characters. Initially, the situation may seem to be similar to Jean-Paul Sartre's *No Exit,* although the characters' reasons for being here are quite different. However, while Sartre's room is clearly in hell, this room can be anywhere. Let the actors investigate and discover—or not discover—their own answers to the riddle. They may get out of this room or discover its significance—or they may not.

This improvisation can be done with the entire class. Tell the students that they are each in the middle of an activity when, suddenly, they find themselves in this strange place with strangers. They also must accept the premise that there is no way out.

History
This play evolved from a photograph of people waiting, which appeared in a brochure for a drama program. Actors from the Metro Theatre Circus in Saint Louis, Missouri, imagined who and where these people were and what they were doing. Metaphorically, the actors were revealing themselves. Emotionally evocative questions were collected, such as: What things in childhood made you afraid? Who was your favorite teacher? What piece of clothing did you hate? The actors wrote autobiographies. The company, along with eight-year-old children, began improvising from these biographies. It was often hard to tell whether the subject was drawn from a child's experience or from an adult's remembrance. Material was gathered from the improvisations for the creation of *In a Room Somewhere*. Suzan Zeder didn't want the actors in the company to play children; she wanted them just to be people in a room somewhere and to identify objects from their own childhood. The play emerged as a composite of remembrances. The actors played themselves and also played parts written by other people. Everything in this play, which took almost four years to develop, was realized improvisationally. The work moved from improvisation to script and now returns to improvisation. By placing *In a Room Somewhere* in this collection of dramatic situations for improvisation, the work has come full circle.

Source: *Katy No-Pocket,* a story by Emmy Payne

Characters
Ensemble; Three females, three males: Katy Kangaroo; Mrs. Crocodile; Mrs. Monkey; Owl; Freddy, Katy's young son; a carpenter

Place
Two locations: a neighborhood in the woods and a city street

Background
Katy Kangaroo had no pocket in which to carry her little boy, Freddy. Distraught, she decided to seek advice from other mothers who managed to transport their children without benefit of pockets.

Situation
Katy and Freddy meet and question first Mrs. Crocodile and then Mrs. Monkey; they learn how each of them carries her children. Katy and

Freddy try both methods, but neither one works. In desperation, they waken the wise old owl, who is slightly deaf. He says that they should go to the city and buy a pocket. So, Katy and Freddy make their way to the city. There they encounter a carpenter wearing an apron with *lots* of pockets, which he kindly gives to Katy.

Comments

The actors playing Mrs. Crocodile, Mrs. Monkey, and Owl can invent their own child-carrying methods, with Katy and Freddy trying unsuccessfully to follow their advice. In the end, the carpenter's apron should provide a solution to their dilemma, although the actors should not feel tied to this resolution if another one occurs logically from the improvisation.

Source: "The Lion, Bruh Bear, and Bruh Rabbit," a folktale told by Virginia Hamilton, in *The People Could Fly*

Characters
Ensemble; Three males or females: Bruh Bear; Bruh Rabbit; Lion

Place
Outside Lion's house in the forest

Background
All the little animals in the forest were afraid to come out of their homes. They were intimidated by Lion, who walked about each day, roaring, "Me and myself. Me and myself." The little animals met and decided to ask for help from Bruh Bear and Bruh Rabbit, who agreed to talk with Lion.

Situation
Bruh Bear and Bruh Rabbit approach Lion and ask him to stop scaring all the little animals. Lion is unmoved by their request. He feels entitled to behave in any way he wants; he is the king of the forest. He is taken aback when Bruh Rabbit tells him that man is the real king of the forest.

Comments
The African-American folktale tradition originated with slaves who were brought to the United States against their will and forced to work under terrible conditions. The slaves created tales out of their experiences, using animals, which took on the characteristics of people, as the principal

characters. The rabbit in these animal tales represents the slave, who knows to fear man.

See also improvisations from the following source: "Doc Rabbit, Bruh Fox, and Tar Baby."

Source: *The Lion, the Witch, and the Wardrobe,* a novel by C.S. Lewis (improvisation written by UCLA student Katriina Hjerppe)

Characters
Ensemble; Two females; two males: Two sisters; two brothers

Place
A room with a big, old wardrobe; during World War II

Background
The four children have been sent to live in a house in the English countryside, away from the bombing in London. An elderly professor owns the house; it is full of curiosities. The most marvelous is the secret entrance to the mysterious and beautiful country of Narnia. The entrance is through the back of an ancient wardrobe, behind a number of old fur coats. Unfortunately, it doesn't always work.

One of the girls found the way by accident when she hid in the closet. She soon discovered that Narnia has no summertime and is ruled by an evil witch. Although the girl thought she had spent many hours in Narnia, she was actually away for only a few seconds.

Situation
The girl has returned from Narnia and is eager to tell everyone about her experience. But her brothers and sister don't believe her. The children go into the wardrobe, but it now is just an ordinary closet. It shows no signs of Narnia. The girl is embarrassed and tries to convince the other children about her fantastic trip, but they make fun of her and say that she's crazy.

Comments
The actress playing the girl must believe that she has just experienced something incredible, the most amazing event in her entire life. She wants to share her discovery and her feelings, but no one will believe what she says. Although the other children tease her, they must also be worried that their sister has gone mad.

Source: "The Mer-Woman out of the Sea," a folktale told by Virginia Hamilton, in *Her Stories: African-American Folktales, Fairy Tales, and True Tales*

Characters
Ensemble; Two males, ensemble: A doctor; Asa, the doctor's helper; townspeople

Place
A coastal area near Charleston, South Carolina; July 3, 1867

Background
It has been raining for nearly five weeks; the city is flooded. There is a rumor circulating that a doctor in town has captured a mermaid. The people come to believe that the rain will not stop until she is set free.

Situation
Asa, the doctor's helper, tells the townspeople that the doctor keeps a "mer-woman being" in a bell jar on the top shelf in a secret room, full of otherworldly creatures. He says that she is beautiful, but she is shrunken because she has been out of the ocean too long. An angry mob gathers outside the doctor's house. They demand that he bring out the mermaid so that they can set her free. The doctor confronts the crowd and explains that there is no mermaid.

Comments
This tale was told by African-American storytellers around the turn of the twentieth century, during a storm that lasted for thirty days. The doctor was never able to convince the angry crowd that he did *not* have a mermaid captured in a jar. Even though they searched the doctor's house, but never found anything, they still blamed him for the endless rains. The doctor had to close his business and move away.

The actors should understand that these people, influenced by their fear of—and lack of control over—nature, believed this story to be true. The actor playing Asa can use his imagination when he describes the mermaid.

Source: *The Mischief Makers*, a play by Lowell Swortzell

Characters
One male, one female: Anansi, a spider; Ano, his wife (played by Raven)

Place
Anansi's home in West Africa

Background
This play is about three famous tricksters: Anansi, the spider; Raven; and Reynard, the fox. Each one claims to be wiser and a better mischief-maker than his competitors. They tell their stories, playing the designated parts for one another.

Anansi believes that he is the wisest creature in the entire animal kingdom. Nyame, the sky god, has a wisdom test, which Anansi wants to take. Nyame laughs at the idea of this little spider, Anansi, thinking that he is so smart. Nyame tries to discourage him from taking the test by telling him that if he fails calamity will befall his family. Anansi, sure that he will pass, is willing to take that chance.

Situation
Anansi tells Ano, his wife (acted by Raven), about the wisdom test, and of the consequences if he fails. Taking the test also means that he has to be away from home for a long period of time. Ano is furious and frightened that the family will be left fatherless. But Anansi has already made a promise to Nyame and cannot renege on it. Ano warns him that tricking a god is not as easy as tricking another spider, but Anansi continues to insist that he is the cleverest of all the creatures, and he departs; he is on his way to take the wisdom test.

Comments
Anansi is an old folk hero; he is known as one of the cleverest animals in mythology. He is conceited and boastful. His argument with his wife is not so different from that of an ordinary couple, arguing about the husband's desire to go off in pursuit of some impossible goal.

See also the following improvisations.

Source: *The Mischief Makers,* a play by Lowell Swortzell

Characters
One male, one female: Anansi, a spider; Ano, his wife (played by Raven)

Place
Anansi's home in West Africa

Background

This play is about three famous tricksters: Anansi, the spider; Raven; and Reynard the fox. Each one claims to be wiser and a better mischief-maker than the other. They tell their stories, playing the designated parts for each other. Anansi believes that he is the wisest creature in the entire animal kingdom. Nyame, the sky god, has a "wisdom" test, which Anansi, against his wife's will, has traveled long and far to take.

Anansi passed the test and is now going back home, after a long absence: he is excited and eager to show his wife all of his new-found sagacity. He has returned with a sheaf of "wisdom"—handwritten notes on scraps of paper. Raven plays the part of Ano, Anansi's wife.

Situation

Anansi proudly shows Ano the scraps of paper, which do not impress her at all. He tells her that he has proved himself to be the wisest creature in the animal kingdom. She replies that all she knows is that he left her and their hungry children to fend for themselves; he doesn't seem any wiser to her. Ano observes, "You may be the wisest creature in Nyame's kingdom, but around here you're just another fast-talking spider" (36–39).

Feeling unappreciated, Anansi vows to keep his wisdom to himself, sealing it in a clay pot. He decides to hide the pot high up in a tree. Ano just laughs at him. Anansi has a hard time climbing the tree with the heavy pot. Ano tells him how to proceed; her wisdom is in her head, not in a pot. When the wind begins to blow, she warns Anansi to come down from the tree. He doesn't heed her warning. The pot falls to the ground and breaks, scattering the notes of wisdom into the air.

Comments

Even Nyame initially laughed at Anansi for thinking that he was the wisest creature. Ano tells him that he is just a speck, looking down from the sky. Perhaps it's because he is so small that he feels the need to prove himself, even at the risk of losing his family. The fun of this piece is in the domestic contrast. Anansi is terribly conceited, his wife remains unimpressed: she turns out to be much wiser than he is, just by staying at home. One nice point of the story is that Anansi cannot keep all the wisdom for himself; he must share it with the world.

The actor playing Raven (who is playing Ano) can have some fun with Anansi. He is probably annoyed by Anansi's bragging and, disguised as Ano, gets back at him by being harsh with the little spider.

See also the following improvisation.

Source: *The Mischief Makers,* a play by Lowell Swortzell

Characters
Ensemble; Two males, one female: An old man (played by Reynard the fox); Raven; the old man's daughter (played by Anansi the spider)

Place
The old man's home in West Africa

Background
This play is about three famous tricksters: Anansi, the spider; Raven; and Reynard, the fox. Each one claims to be the wisest creature in the animal kingdom. They have a contest in which each tells a story about how he outwitted another creature. This is Raven's tale.

There once was an old man who had all the light in the world closed up in a box. He would never relinquish the light, and all the world was in darkness. Raven decided to trick the old man and steal the light.

Situation
The old man and his daughter are having dinner. Raven appears and tries to talk them into letting light into the world, using the argument that the man will be able to see his daughter's beauty. The old man insists that he has no light. Raven says that he has heard there is a ball of light hidden in a small box in this very house. Raven is tired of having to do everything in the dark; he begs for light, but to no avail. The old man tells him to leave. Raven warns him that he will find a way to get the light—by trickery.

Comments
The actor playing Raven should use his ingenuity to get the light. The actor portraying the old man must have a strong reason for not letting light into the world.

In this tale, Raven has the ability to transform himself into many different natural forms. This time, he chooses to become a pine needle in a pond. When the daughter swallows him in a mouthful of water, he becomes a fetus in her stomach and is born a baby boy. The old man adores the baby and will let him do anything. The baby boy insists that he wants to play with the boxes. The old man reluctantly agrees, warning him not to open the very last box (which contains the ball of light). But, the boy does open it, letting light into the world. He instantly changes back into Raven—and lets his trickery be known. The actors may want to include the above as part two of the improvisation.

See also the preceding improvisations.

Source: *Mr. Popper's Penguins,* a novel by Richard and Florence Atwater

Characters
Ensemble; Two females, two males, one male or female: Jane, a nine-year-old girl; Bill, her twelve-year-old brother; Mr. and Mrs. Popper, their parents; a penguin

Place
The Poppers' living room, Stillwater, USA

Background
Mr. Popper, a house painter by trade, has a fascination (shared by the rest of the family) with the Antarctic. After Admiral Drake, who was on an expedition to the South Pole, received a letter from Mr. Popper, he sent back a surprise in response. It has just been delivered to the Popper residence in a large crate by air express.

Situation
Mr. Popper calls everyone—Mrs. Popper, Jane, and Bill—to see the large crate sent by Admiral Drake all the way from the South Pole. They have no idea what it contains. They open the crate—and out walks a penguin!

Comments
The actors should communicate their utter amazement at having a penguin suddenly appear in their home. As the penguin begins to explore the house and its contents, eventually finding a place for itself in the refrigerator, the actors will experience and express a number of different reactions. At no time should there be the slightest sense that this is "business as usual" at the Poppers' house. The actor playing the penguin may want to study the movements and sounds of an actual penguin before doing this improvisation.

Source: *The Native American Cinderella,* a play by Lowell Swortzell, in *Cinderella, The World's Favorite Fairy Tale*

Characters
Ensemble; Four females: Broken Wing; Blue Fox, her elder sister; Grey Seal, the next to eldest sister; Morning Star, sister of the Invisible Hunter

Place
The wigwam of Morning Star and the Invisible Hunter

Background

Caribou lived in a wigwam with his three daughters, Broken Wing, Blue Fox, and Grey Seal. He was away for long periods of time, trading furs with other tribes. The girls' mother had died many years ago. They were part of the Micmac tribe, living on ancient land, which today is called Nova Scotia.

Broken Wing was the youngest daughter. She had burn scars on her face. Blue Fox, her elder sister, called her "scarface." She made Broken Wing wait on her hand and foot. She did cruel things to her sister, such as forcing her to hold her hand in the fire. Grey Seal, the other sister, tried to dissuade Blue Fox from mistreating Broken Wing, but to no avail.

Morning Star dwelt in a wigwam nearby with her brother, a great hunter. He was invisible to everyone except to her. The legend was that only a maiden who could see him could marry him. Morning Star gave the young ladies a test, which many took and failed. Blue Fox was preparing to become the Invisible Hunter's wife; Broken Wing was helping her. Caribou encouraged Broken Wing to take the test, too, but she believed that she was too ugly because of the burns on her face. At last, he did convince her to go.

Situation

This situation takes place when Blue Fox and Grey Seal arrive at the wigwam of Morning Star and the Invisible Hunter. Morning Star admires Blue Fox's necklace, which was made by Broken Wing. She asks to see Broken Wing, but Blue Fox insists that her "scarface" sister is too ugly to look at. Morning Star gives Blue Fox the test, asking her such questions as what she sees beyond the trees, and what the Invisible Hunter's shoulder strap and bow strings are made of. Blue Fox answers every question incorrectly, although she pretends that she can see the hunter. Grey Fox does not take the test because she says that she cannot see anything. Morning Star tells them she is waiting for another maiden to be tested, and asks them to please leave. As they depart, they see, much to their surprise, that the next person is Broken Wing. And when Morning Star puts questions to her, she answers them all correctly. She has passed the test! Broken Wing will marry the Invisible Hunter.

Comments

The actors should create their own questions and answers regarding the Invisible Hunter. Blue Fox is selfish and unkind to Broken Wing, but she is very unhappy with her life and desperately wants to get out of the house. She sees the Invisible Hunter as her salvation; her sadness makes her ruthless. Broken Wing's answers are of a spiritual nature. The Invisible Hunter is never seen by the audience, but his voice is heard when he speaks with Broken Wing, who has now become beautiful.

See also improvisations from the following sources: *Cinderella in China, The Russian Cinderella,* and *The Rough-Face Girl.*

Source: *Nightingale,* a play for children, adapted by John Urquhart and Rita Grossberg, from the story by Hans Christian Andersen

Characters
One male, one female: the Emperor of China; the nightingale

Place
The emperor's palace

Background
Nothing could make the emperor happy. He had the most beautiful palace in the world, splendid flower gardens, the finest robes, but he always wanted more. Eventually, his attitude angered the gods, and they destroyed what they had given him. The emperor grew more and more melancholy, and the people of China were sad that their emperor was so unhappy. He ordered music, but kept demanding more and more instruments until there were no more. Finally, a servant brought him a nightingale. This nightingale told the servant that the emperor would be happy if he listened to the nightingale's song in his own heart.

Situation
The emperor, happy again after hearing the nightingale sing, ties her feet so that she cannot escape. She pleads with him to let her go, claiming that she cannot sing with her feet tied. However, the emperor refuses to untie her; he thinks her song belongs among the splendors of his court, not in the forest. He orders fancy robes for her, which only weigh her down; she needs only her feathers. She begs him to remove the robes, but he refuses.

The emperor invites the people of China to hear the nightingale sing. He announces that they are about to hear the most beautiful song. She attempts to sing, but only a melancholy sound comes out. Without freedom, she cannot sing.

Comments
The audience can serve as the people of China. In the play, the emperor has the nightingale banned from all of China; only when he is dying from sadness does the nightingale return to sing for him and to revive him. This story parallels many present-day relationships and situations: parent/child; husband/wife; boyfriend/girlfriend; caging a wild animal for a pet. The emperor

is afraid of losing the only thing that makes him happy, but the nightingale cannot deliver as long as she is a prisoner. The actor playing the emperor must be in touch with his fear and selfishness. It is a dilemma for the emperor.

Source: "The Other Frog Prince," a story by Jon Scieszka and Lane Smith, in *The Stinky Cheese Man and Other Fairly Stupid Tales*

Characters
One male, one female: A frog; a beautiful princess

Place
A lily pond

Situation
A frog sees a beautiful princess sitting by the pond. He hops out of the water and tells her that he needs her help. He claims that he is not really a frog, but he is a handsome prince who was turned into a frog by a wicked witch's spell. The spell can be broken only by the kiss of a beautiful princess. The princess wonders what to do. She's a little frightened hearing a frog talk, and she is not sure if she believes him. It turns out that the frog is lying; he's really only a frog trying to get kissed.

Comments
The actor playing the princess can decide whether or not she wants to kiss the frog. It depends on how convincing he is about his need to be rescued. If she does kiss him, she needs to deal with how she feels about being tricked by a frog. The actor playing the frog has to be willing to make the physical and vocal commitment. Also, he must find a strong reason for playing this trick. Maybe he's lonely or he hates beautiful princesses or he really believes he *is* a prince. However, he does not change into a man. Since this is fantasy, there are all kinds of possibilities.

Source: *Peter Pan,* a novel by James M. Barrie

Characters
One female, one male: Wendy Darling, ten years old; Peter Pan, ageless

Place
Wendy's bedroom, in her family's home, London, England

Background
Peter Pan left home the day he was born because he wanted to be a little boy, always, and never grow up. He ran away to Kensington Gardens and lived among the fairies. Wendy is a little girl who lives a normal life with her family. Her mother read the story of Cinderella to her just before Wendy went to sleep for the night.

Situation
Wendy awakens to find Peter Pan. He is at the foot of her bed, crying because he has lost his shadow. Wendy helps him to find it and sews it back on for him. Peter then tells her that he lives with a group of lost boys and that they need a girl to tell them stories. He wants to teach Wendy how to fly so that they can fly together.

Comments
The actor playing Wendy must accept her character's belief in fairies. Also, she does not feel as one would today upon awakening to find a stranger in one's bedroom. Wendy's life is not very exciting, and Peter offers her much excitement. But Peter must entice Wendy, not frighten her. He needs her company, and there is a reason for his choice of her (which the actor may discover). Wendy would have to give up the security of her home, which is not easy; even at the age of ten it's scary to go off with a stranger in the middle of the night—to "fly." She may decide not to go. (The actors need not feel compelled to follow the story line of *Peter Pan* exactly.)

Extra characters may be added, for example, Tinkerbell and Peter's shadow. The shadow is a good role for a nonverbal child. The children can fly around the room as the teacher asks them what they see from up there. Have them describe it afterwards. Discussion can follow, especially about the difference between reality and fantasy.

See index for other improvisations from this source.

Source: *Pippi Longstocking,* a book by Astrid Lindgren

Characters
Ensemble; Two females, one male: Pippi Longstocking, a nine-year-old girl; Amanda, a neighbor; Tommy, a neighbor

Place
Villa Villekula, a house in a garden at the edge of a village

Background
Pippi's mother died when Pippi was just an infant. So the young girl grew up aboard a ship with her sea captain father. When her father was blown overboard in a storm, Pippi went to live at Villa Villekula, the home her father had bought for his retirement. She took along a little monkey named Mr. Nilssen—and a suitcase full of gold pieces. Tommy and Amanda live in the house next door.

Situation
Tommy and Amanda, who are very well-behaved children, were away when Pippi moved in, so they are taken by surprise when she appears. Her big red braids sticking straight out, her unconventional manner of dress, and her monkey sitting on her shoulder, make her quite a curious figure. Tommy and Amanda are delighted when she invites them in for breakfast. Pippi makes pancakes for her guests in the most outlandish way imaginable.

Comments
The actor playing Pippi should behave as outrageously as possible with no apparent regard for, or realization of, the impact her acting has on her guests. Tommy and Amanda are simultaneously delighted with—and horrified by—Pippi.

Source: *A Por Quinly Christmas,* a play by Quincy Long

Characters
One male, one female or male: Por Quinly, a young boy; a Christmas tree

Place
The living room of Por Quinly's home; Christmas Eve

Background
Por Quinly's mother has been telling him to go to bed so that Santa Claus can come.

Situation
Por Quinly is writing something to himself when, all of a sudden, the Christmas tree begins to talk to him. At first, he has no idea where the voice is coming from, but then he realizes that the tree is speaking.

Comments
The actor playing the tree should decide for herself why she is talking to Por

Quinly and what she is saying. What does she want from him? Por Quinly, never having experienced a talking tree before, has no idea how to react. He may be frightened, he may be amused. It is definitely a surprise.

Source: "The Princess of the Sea," a story by Robin Hall, in *Three Tales From Japan*

Characters
One male, one female: Urashima Taro, a fisherman; an old woman

Place
A fishing village in Japan

Background
Some children were tormenting a tortoise, when Urashima, the best fisherman in the village, rescued it. The tortoise was actually a princess in disguise. Each year, the Dragon King required his daughter to assume the guise of a lowly creature and move about on earth to test men's kindness. As a reward for his kindness, Urashima was given the Box of the Dragon Claw to guard him on his way—but he was never to open it!

Situation
Three days later, Urashima returns from the sea to his village. Strangely enough, nobody recognizes him, and he does not recognize anyone. And even though it is a small village, where everybody knows each other, his name is unknown to the villagers. An old woman says that she has lived here all of her life but has never heard of him. As they talk, she recalls stories of a boy named Urashima Taro, a fisherman who went out to sea three hundred years ago. Urashima suddenly realizes that he must have opened the box when he was given it three days ago, and that three days in the land of the Dragon King must be equivalent to three hundred years on earth.

Comments
This is a major discovery for Urashima—he thought that only three days had passed since he rescued the tortoise and was given the box. It will take time for him to absorb what has happened. He must visualize where he was when he opened the box, then figure out why he opened it. The actor might improvise some moments from the fisherman's past before attempting this situation. Have him be specific about Urashima's family, friends, business people, teachers, pets.

Source: *The Rat and the Lion*, a fable, as told by Nigerian storyteller Ndubisi Nwafor Ejelimna to Sandra Caruso (1996)

Characters
Ensemble; One female, two males: Mother Rat; Baby Rat; a lion

Place
The Nigerian bush

Background
Baby Rat has not yet learned to obey Mother Rat's sound advice. Mother Rat has told Baby Rat not to venture out into the bush at noontime, because of the danger from big, wild beasts. But, right now, Mother Rat is fast asleep and snoring, so Baby Rat sneaks out for a reckless ramble in the bush in search of nuts.

Situation
The lion is having a good nap after a heavy meal of antelope. Baby Rat, who is rustling around in the grass and fallen leaves, unwittingly strays into the mane of the sleeping lion, mistaking it for a heap of brown grass. The lion wakes up, feels something in his mane and plucks out the little rat. Baby Rat frets, and quakes, and trembles in fear. He begs for forgiveness. The lion lets Baby Rat go because he is already full. (Besides, the little rat would not even make a good mouthful.)

Comments
This is a fable and therefore has a moral: the powerful can also be kind to the weak. This is also a clear lesson about the dangers of disobedience.

Source: "La Rebelion de los Conejos Magicos" (The rebellion of the magical rabbits), a short story by Ariel Dorfman, in *Where Angels Glide at Dawn: New Stories from Latin America*, edited by Lori M. Carlson and Cynthia L. Ventura

Characters
One male, one female: A monkey; his young daughter

Place
The daughter's bedroom; early morning

Background
The wolves conquered the land of the rabbits. Their king proclaimed that

rabbits had ceased to exist; it was forbidden to even mention the word *rabbit*. A monkey, who was a photographer, was hired by the king to document with his camera each important event in the king's life.

Situation
The monkey is about to leave for work at the palace when his daughter stops him. She loves rabbits and asks her father to take some pictures of them for her. She tells him that the rabbits used to come to visit her, but that they don't anymore. (The rabbits have gone into hiding.) The monkey becomes very upset; it is illegal to even talk about rabbits, and the penalty for breaking the law is death. So, although he knows in his heart that they do exist, he insists that rabbits do not exist. He must lie to his child to save their lives.

Comments
The monkey's daughter has a passion for rabbits. To her father, denying their existence is the same as denying her happiness. The actors must accept as a given that, in a dictatorship, it is dangerous to discuss forbidden subjects even in the privacy of your own home. You never know who might be listening. The actors may choose to play this scene as human beings rather than as monkeys. Also, if they wish, they may substitute another animal for rabbits.

Source: *The Russian Cinderella,* a play by Lowell Swortzell, in *Cinderella, The World's Favorite Fairy Tale*

Characters
Two females: Vasilisa, a young girl; Baba Yaga, a witch

Place
Baba Yaga's house in Russia

Background
Vasilisa's mother was dead, and her father was away in distant lands. Her stepmother and two stepsisters made her do all the work. One day, a doll—one that her mother had given to her—spoke to Vasilisa and told her that she would help with her chores.

News of Vasilisa's beauty spread throughout the countryside and a young man came to the house to see *her*, instead of her stepsisters. They were so angry that the stepmother decided to get rid of Vasilisa by sending her to Baba Yaga, the witch, who eats children. Vasilisa was sent to the witch's house with the pretext of borrowing a candle. Vasilisa took her doll with her. When they arrived at the home of Baba Yaga, the witch, who was going out, gave Vasilisa an impossible number of tasks to be done by the time she returned. Vasilisa, with the help of her magical doll, completed all of the work.

Situation

Baba Yaga returns and is amazed to find everything done. When Vasilisa tells her that the doll did it, Baba Yaga says that she'll let Vasilisa go—if she leaves the doll. Vasilisa refuses to give up the doll. Baba Yaga becomes angry; she can't understand why Vasilisa won't sacrifice this toy in exchange for her life. Vasilisa tells Baba Yaga that her mother gave her the doll with her blessing; that's why she loves it so much. This makes Baba Yaga furious. When Vasilisa asks her why she's so angry, the witch explains that love destroys her magical powers.

Comments

As the fairy tale continues, when Baba Yaga can't convince Vasilisa to leave her doll, the witch still lets her go before she—Baba Yaga—is destroyed by love. Although Baba Yaga is an out-and-out evil character, the actors might find an alternative ending, in which Baba Yaga changes her attitude.

Baba Yaga was a wicked witch who appeared in many Russian folktales. She was known for devouring children; she lived in a house raised up from the ground on chicken legs; she possessed great wicked magical powers—but the presence of love undid them.

See also improvisations from the following sources: *Cinderella in China*, *The Native American Cinderella*, and *The Rough-Face Girl*.

Source: *Stuart Little,* a novel by E.B. White

Characters

One male, one female: Stuart Little, a mouse; Harriet Ames, a young girl of diminutive stature

Place

Ames Landing, on a river bank in Ames Crossing, Connecticut

Background

Stuart Little left the comfort of his family in New York City to go out into the world to search for his friend, Margalo, and to seek his fortune. On his journey, he stopped in the town of Ames Crossing, where a storekeeper told him about Harriet Ames, a petite young person just about Stuart's size. A chance encounter with Harriet prompted Stuart to invite her for a canoe ride.

Situation
Stuart arrives at Ames Landing with a canoe, which he moors to the bank. As he talks to himself about his impending date, the canoe behind him becomes untied and drifts away. Soon after, Harriet arrives. After greetings and pleasantries are exchanged, Stuart looks around and realizes that the canoe is gone. Harriet suggests other things they might do, but Stuart is not to be consoled. On an awkward note, Harriet leaves.

Comments
Stuart can't get beyond his own frustration and disappointment; he can't enjoy his time with Harriet in any other way than the way he had imagined it. Harriet tries to save the situation by offering other alternatives, but she knows better than to beat a dead horse.

See index for other improvisations from this source.

Source: *Swimmy,* a story by Leo Lionni

Characters
Ensemble; Any number of males and females: Swimmy, a little black fish; a giant tuna fish; a medusa; a lobster; sea anemones; a strange fish; a forest of seaweed; an eel; a school of little red fish

Place
Under the sea

Background
A school of little red fish lived happily in the sea, until the tuna fish swallowed them all—except for Swimmy. Scared, lonely, and very sad, Swimmy began to cheer up as he swam about, discovering the beauty of the sea and meeting many intriguing underwater creatures. Finally, he met a school of little red fish just like the one he had lost.

Situation
Swimmy is delighted to find the new school of fish. He wants the little fish to leave their hiding place and swim with him, playing and enjoying the wonders of the sea. However, the little fish are afraid that the tuna will see them and eat them. Swimmy uses his imagination both to rally the fish

and to solve the problem. He teaches them to swim together in the shape of one giant fish, and they chase the tuna away. The little fish are jubilant in their victory.

Comments
It is Swimmy's ability to imagine a solution to the problem that allows the fish to confront the tuna. It is the well-orchestrated, cooperative effort of the little fish working together as a single unit that defeats the big and powerful enemy. This is a good improvisation for creative movement.

Source: *The Tale of Jemima Puddle Duck,* a story by Beatrix Potter

Characters
One female, one male: Jemima, a duck; a good-looking stranger, a fox

Place
The middle of the woods

Background
Unhappy that she was never allowed to hatch her own eggs, Jemima Puddle Duck decided to make her nest outside, away from the farm yard. She was exploring the woods for a suitable nest site, when she encountered a well-dressed stranger who is, in fact, a fox.

Situation
The fox expresses his eagerness to help Jemima find a place to make a nest. Grateful, Jemima has no idea that an ulterior motive lurks behind this stranger's kind behavior.

Comments
Jemima is a true innocent—and more than a little simple-minded. The fox is a classically evil character, conniving and manipulative through-and-through. In Beatrix Potter's story, the farmer's dog, Kip, saves the day, but the actors may resolve the situation in any way they wish.

Source: *The Tale of Peter Rabbit,* a story by Beatrix Potter

Characters
Two males: Peter, a rabbit; Mr. McGregor, a gardener

Place
Mr. McGregor's garden

Background
Flopsy, Mopsy, Cottontail, and Peter lived with their mother, Mrs. Rabbit, under a big tree. Mrs. Rabbit has told her children that they can go to the fields or down the lane, but that they must never go into Mr. McGregor's garden.

Situation
Leaving his siblings behind, Peter disobeys and squeezes under the gate into Mr. McGregor's garden. He feasts on lettuce, French beans, and radishes with great delight until he comes upon Mr. McGregor working in the garden. Spying this intruder, Mr. McGregor chases him—and Peter runs for his life.

Comments
The situation is played best without words, using only vocalizations. It should consist of a great chase, with many near catches, and can be resolved in any way that seems realistic to the actors.

Source: *The Tale of the Shining Princess,* a Japanese tale, adapted by Sally Fisher from a translation of the story by Donald Keene

Characters
One female, one male: Princess Kaguya-Lime; the emperor

Place
Outside Kaguya-Lime's home in a small village in Japan; the ninth or tenth century A.D.

Background
A bamboo cutter found a tiny girl, just three inches tall, in a bamboo stalk. He brought her home to his wife, and the couple decided to adopt her. They did not know that she was the Princess Kaguya-Lime from the Palace of the Moon, a magical and unearthly being.

The couple fed her well; and in three months she grew to normal adult stature. Her beauty attracted many suitors, but Kaguya-Lime knew that she could not marry a mortal. Therefore she told her suitors that before she accepted a proposal from any man, he must complete certain tasks

(designed by her to be impossible to fulfill). At last, the emperor sent for
Kaguya-Lime. She had no choice but to obey his summons.

Situation
The emperor and Kaguya-Lime meet and fall in love immediately. However, she must find a way to tell him that she is no ordinary mortal.
Kaguya-Lime doesn't want the emperor to feel rejected because she loves
him. But she must make him understand why they cannot be married.

Comments
In the story, Kaguya-Lime turns herself into a ball of light to prove that
she is not of this world. The actor can devise her own way of demonstrat-
ing this.

See also the following improvisation.

Source: *The Tale of the Shining Princess,* a Japanese tale, adapted by Sally Fisher from a translation of the story by Donald Keene

Characters
Ensemble; Two females, one male: Princess Kaguya-Lime; her earth parents

Place
Outside the princess' home in a small village in Japan; the ninth or tenth
century A.D.

Background
A bamboo cutter found a tiny girl, just three inches tall, in a bamboo shoot,
and brought her home to his wife. Under their care, Kaguya-Lime grew into
a beautiful woman of full stature. Her parents know nothing of her origins,
but they have come to love her as their own child. Lately, Kaguya-Lime has
become melancholy. Her parents often find her gazing at the moon.

Situation
Kaguya-Lime's parents ask her what is wrong. Weeping, she tells them
that she is sad and lonely; the world seems a dreary place. They beg her
to tell them the cause of her sorrow. Kaguya-Lime reveals that she is not
from the earth; she is from the Palace of the Moon. She was sent to earth
as a punishment for something that she did a long time ago. She wasn't

supposed to stay here so long, but she loved the man and his wife so much that she could not bear to leave. But, she has a mother and father in the Palace of the Moon who want her to return. She has not thought of them while here on earth. The bamboo cutter and his wife are grief-stricken: Kaguya-Lime has become their child. They plead with her not to leave them. She tells them that the immortals have the power to take her. Her earth parents can do nothing to stop them.

At last, Kaguya-Lime tells the bamboo cutter and his wife that she must ascend into the sky. The immortals are urging her to put on the celestial robe of forgetfulness, made of feathers, and return to them. Once she dons the robe, she will lose her earthly emotions. She assures her parents that she loves them; however, the moment she puts on the celestial robe of forgetfulness, it will all be over. Sorrowfully, she draws the robe of feathers over her shoulders. Then her unhappiness leaves her, and she no longer remembers anything about her life on earth. In her magical robe of feathers she rises into the sky, transformed into a bird.

Comments

This last moment of transformation is very theatrical and demands that the actor incorporate her whole body. The entire class could do this exercise. Tell them the story and have them say good-bye to loved ones, change into a bird, and return to the moon. The emperor can also be present in this last scene.

See also the preceding improvisation.

Source: *Tuck Everlasting,* a novel by Natalie Babbitt

Characters

One female, one male: Winnie Foster, a ten-year-old girl, going on eleven; Jesse Tuck, a seventeen-year-old boy

Place

Wooded land owned by Winnie Foster's family, on the outskirts of the village of Treegap

Background

Winnie Foster, an only child, was bored with her life. Tired of always being told what to do, she ran away to the woods, where she met Jesse Tuck. Winnie was immediately and wholeheartedly attracted to Jesse, as she watched him drink water from an underground spring.

This was the very spring from which Jesse and the rest of his family drank eighty-seven years ago; its magical waters gave them eternal life. Jesse realized that Winnie had been watching him. They introduced themselves and Winnie began to question Jesse. Winnie and Jesse were both extremely lonely in their own ways. They began to get to know each other and to enjoy each other's company. In the midst of the conversation, Winnie became thirsty and asked for a drink of water from the spring.

Situation
Jesse can't let Winnie drink from the spring or tell her the real reason why she cannot. The more adamant Jesse is that she cannot touch the water, the more determined Winnie is to have a drink.

Comments
Jesse must be aware of the implications of drinking from the spring and believe it is absolutely imperative that he keep Winnie from drinking. At the same time, Winnie must take control of her own life and stand up to authority. Besides, Jesse just drank from the spring; why can't she? After all, it's more *her* spring than Jesse's—it's on land owned by her parents!

See also the following improvisation.

Source: *Tuck Everlasting,* a novel by Natalie Babbitt

Characters
Ensemble; Two females, two males: Winnie Foster, ten years old; Jesse Tuck, seventeen years old; Mr. and Mrs. Tuck, the parents of Jesse

Place
Wooded land owned by Winnie Foster's family on the outskirts of the village of Treegap

Background
Eighty-seven years ago the Tuck family arrived in Treegap, looking for a place to settle. After drinking water from a spring in the woods near Treegap, the Tucks stopped aging. As time passed, their friends and neighbors began to avoid the family, because while all the village people grew older, the Tucks never changed. The villagers suspected black magic.

One day, Winnie Foster, a young girl from Treegap who was bored with her life, ran away to the woods. She met the Tucks' youngest son, Jesse, who stopped her from drinking the waters of the spring. The Tucks then kidnapped Winnie and brought her to their home deep in the woods.

Situation

The Tucks explain to Winnie that they had to kidnap her—to keep the rest of the world from learning of their whereabouts. When Winnie fully understands the Tucks' reasoning, they will take her back home. Mr. Tuck says that if people knew about the spring in Treegap, "they'd all come running like pigs to slops. They'd trample each other, trying to get some water" (64). He predicts what the world would be like if everybody lived forever; that people just wouldn't realize the terrible consequences of immortality until it would be too late.

Comments

This is a strange story that the Tucks relate to Winnie. It sounds like a fairy tale. Winnie has to decide whether to believe it. This is certainly not her idea of what being kidnapped would be like; the Tucks are very kind to her. (Of course, they might be crazy.) The actors should give some thought to the isolated life that the Tucks have led all these years and how happy they might be to keep Winnie with them. They cannot release her until they are confident that she understands the full significance of their secret.

In Natalie Babbitt's novel, a man in a yellow suit tracks Winnie to the Tucks' home. He is determined to return her to her home. He realizes what has happened to the Tucks, and he tells them that he intends to spread the news about the spring and charge people money to drink its waters. Winnie and the Tucks know he has to be stopped. What they decide to do could be the basis for another improvisation.

See also the preceding improvisation.

Source: *Two Foolish Goats and a Monkey,* a fable as told by Nigerian storyteller Ndubisi Nwafor Ejelimna to Sandra Caruso (1996)

Characters

Ensemble; Three males or females: Two goats; a monkey

Place

A village pathway in Nigeria

Background

Two goats were grazing along the village pathway when they found one *naira* (the Nigerian unit of currency, equal to one United States dollar) on the ground. They argued and quarreled about how to divide the single bill into two shares. A monkey, on his way to the market, heard them arguing. When he learned what the dispute was about, he suggested that the best solution would be to go to a nearby bakery, buy a loaf of bread, and share it in equal parts. The goats liked this idea and gave the *naira* to the monkey, who went off on his errand.

Situation
The monkey returns with the bread. Since he has shown himself to be wise and friendly, the goats ask him to break the loaf into equal parts for them. The monkey then begins his trickery. He cuts the loaf into two unequal parts. The goats point out that the pieces are uneven. The monkey takes a big bite from the bigger half and the *other* half becomes bigger. Again the goats ask the monkey to try to make the two halves equal in size; again the monkey takes a big bite from the larger half and swallows it. The goats observe that the halves are *still* unequal. The monkey continues to take bites from each piece, until the whole loaf is gone.

Comments
This is a fable and, therefore, has a moral: if you are too foolish to take care of yourself, someone else will take advantage of your foolishness. Let the students attempt to discover the moral first.

Source: *The Velveteen Rabbit,* a story by Margery Williams

Characters
Ensemble; Three males or females: the velveteen rabbit, a stuffed toy; two real rabbits

Place
The woods

Background
The velveteen rabbit has become the boy's favorite toy and constant companion. The rabbit believes himself to be real because of the nursery magic that defines "real" not as how you are made, but as the authenticity that comes from being loved by a child.

Situation
The velveteen rabbit waits in his cozy nest in the woods while the boy wanders off to pick flowers. Two wild rabbits appear out of the woods. They are as curious about the velveteen rabbit as he is about them. The two wild rabbits invite him to play with them, but, of course, he is unable to move.

Comments
This situation allows for an interesting exploration of movement revealed by the contrast between the real and the stuffed animals. The dialogue among the rabbits may lead, as it does in the story, to considerations of what makes something real. Regardless, the emotions beneath the dialogue are real and the actors must believe the premise of the story.

Source: *Where the Wild Things Are,* a story by Maurice Sendak

Characters
Ensemble; Any number of males and females

Place
Where the wild things are

Background
Max was sent to bed because he had been making mischief. He fell asleep and dreamed that he was sailing off in a boat to the place where the wild things live.

Situation
Max meets up with the wild things. They interact until Max decides it's time to go home.

Comments
In the book, the wild things are ferocious, rolling their eyes, baring their teeth, and roaring loudly. Max is frightened of the wild things until he tames them, at which point they all carry on and have a fine time together. However, the actors can choose to have the encounter go in any direction that feels true.

Source: *Winnie-the-Pooh,* a book by A.A. Milne

Characters
Ensemble; Three males or females: Winnie-the-Pooh, a bear; Christopher Robin, his friend; Rabbit; Rabbit's friends and relations (optional)

Place
Rabbit's home in the Hundred Acre Wood

Background

Out for a walk in the woods, Winnie-the-Pooh decided to stop in and visit his friend, Rabbit. He pushed his way down through the hole leading into Rabbit's home. Rabbit served his guest a sumptuous spread, which Pooh thoroughly enjoyed.

Situation

Pooh tries to leave Rabbit's house by the front door, only to discover that he has eaten so much food that he can't fit all the way through the hole. It quickly becomes apparent that Pooh is stuck—he can't move forward or backward. At his wit's end, Rabbit prevails upon Christopher Robin to come to their rescue.

Comments

In Milne's book, Christopher Robin has Pooh fast for a week. Then, Christopher Robin, Rabbit, and Rabbit's friends and relations form a long line and pull Pooh out. The actors may use this strategy, or they may invent other strategies to extricate Pooh. The focus should be on finding a solution to Pooh's dilemma, while he gives instructions to his rescuers.

Source: *The Wizard of Oz,* a novel by L. Frank Baum

Characters

Ensemble; Two females, four males or females: Dorothy, a young girl; the Good Witch of the North; Munchkins; Toto, Dorothy's dog

Place

The Land of Oz

Background

A cyclone carried Dorothy's home (along with Dorothy and her dog, Toto) from Kansas, where she lived with her Aunt Em and Uncle Henry, to the Land of Oz.

Situation

Dorothy opens the front door of her house and finds that she is in an entirely new place. The Good Witch of the North, an older woman dressed in white, accompanied by three Munchkins, tiny creatures dressed in blue, approach her. They hail Dorothy as a heroine—her house landed on top of the Wicked Witch of the East, an evil woman who held the Munchkins as her slaves, and killed her! Dorothy, eager to find her way back to Kansas, is directed to the Great Wizard, who lives in the Emerald City.

Comments

The actors probably will know the story. However, they need not follow the established story line. The focus for the actor playing Dorothy will be on her initial reaction to an unfamiliar place and then on her desire to find her way back home. The Munchkins and the Good Witch of the North will show Dorothy their gratitude and admiration. And, remember, Dorothy is as strange to them as they are to her.

4

Relationship

This chapter focuses on situations in which the primary element is the relationship between two characters. If it is a long-standing relationship, the actors should research the history of these people to discover what they like or dislike about each other. The relationship between two people in a scene is about much more than the factual connection or the formal arrangements between them. It is about the multiplicity of feelings in the relationship—the full emotional attitude of each character toward the other character. Also, it is useful to endow other characters with a secret—something you know about them that they do not know you know. It is these kinds of background details that will determine the ways in which characters relate to one another truthfully.

Milton Katselas once told an acting class that all relationships must be Clytemnestra and Agamemnon. It is not all simple reality; it is also a Greek chorus. The relationships in this chapter must all be approached with that sense of importance. These characters' lives are interwoven with and crucial to each other. The actors must concentrate on each other. They cannot simply stand alone and talk.

Love is an element in all relationships, even if it is only the *desire* to love and to be loved. In *Audition*, Michael Shurtleff writes that love is a "given" in every scene; characters always want love from each other. The actor should learn which kind of love is present in the relationship—passionate, familial, obsessive, spiritual, affectionate—and how it affects the interactions of the characters. "The desire for love, to give it or receive it and preferably both and simultaneously, is the chief propellant in human beings. An actor had best learn that love comes in all forms, and in many more forms than only those he himself admires" (Shurtleff 1978, 29).

RELATIONSHIP SITUATIONS

One male, one female
Charlotte's Web

Fly Away Home

A Little Princess

Stuart Little

Two females
Addy Learns a Lesson

Addy Saves the Day

Meet the Austins

Two males
Ira Sleeps Over

Justin and the Best Biscuits in the World

Slow Dance

A Very Special Kwanzaa

Ensemble
The Kid

M Butterfly

The Secret Garden

Tales of a Fourth Grade Nothing

Tom Sawyer

Source: *Addy Learns a Lesson,* a novel by Connie Porter

Characters

Two females: Addy Walker, a nine-year-old black girl; Sarah Moore, a nine-year-old white girl

Place

Philadelphia, Pennsylvania; the late 1860s

Background

Addy and her mother escaped from their lives as plantation slaves in North Carolina and arrived in Philadelphia as free people. They were soon be-friended by Sarah Moore and her mother. Sarah took Addy to school with her, where Addy became enchanted by Harriet, the indulged leader of an exclusive group of girls. Addy tried to be friends with both Sarah and Harriet for a little while, but, quickly engulfed by the wonders of Harriet's luxurious life, forsook Sarah.

Situation
Addy has realized that Harriet is neither a good person nor a true friend. She sees that her attraction to Harriet was merely superficial, and she feels remorse that she hurt Sarah. Addy goes to Sarah to apologize, to beg her forgiveness, and to ask her to consider being friends again.

Comments
Addy has learned an important lesson about friendship. (The actor playing Addy can decide which event or events led to her change of heart about Harriet.) She is truly sorry for the way in which she has treated Sarah. The actor playing Sarah must decide if she can find it in her heart to forgive Addy for hurting her—and if she will be able to trust her as a friend in the future.

See also improvisations from the following sources: *Meet Addy, Addy's Surprise, Happy Birthday Addy!, Addy Saves the Day,* and *Changes for Addy.*

Source: *Addy Saves the Day,* a novel by Connie Porter

Characters
Two females: Addy Walker, a ten-year-old girl; Harriet Davis, a ten-year-old girl

Place
A sabbath school room at Trinity American Methodist Episcopal Church in Philadelphia, Pennsylvania; the late nineteenth century

Background
The Civil War is over. Many of the churches in Philadelphia have joined together to sponsor a fair to raise money for people hurt by the war. The children were to come up with their own fund-raising project. Addy found herself having to work with Harriet Davis, her snobby desk partner from school. A disagreement about what the children's project should be rekindles their old feud. Neither girl wants to work with the other.

Situation
It is the day of the fair. Addy runs inside the sabbath school classroom to get a basket, and she hears someone crying. Following the sound, she discovers Harriet in the broom closet. Addy tries to find out what is wrong, but Harriet is sobbing too hard to respond. Finally, Harriet is able to say

that her beloved uncle has died. Addy feels great compassion for Harriet and reaches out to console her.

Comments
In the book, the tragedy allows both girls to be more understanding of one another and to see what they have in common. The actor playing Harriet must feel the effect Harriet's loss has in making her vulnerable to Addy's real concern and empathy. Both girls are changed by this interaction.

See also improvisations from the following sources: *Meet Addy, Addy Learns a Lesson, Addy's Surprise, Happy Birthday Addy,* and *Changes for Addy.*

Source: *Charlotte's Web,* a novel by E.B. White

Characters
One male, one female: Wilbur, a pig; Charlotte, a spider

Place
Wilbur's pen at the county fairgrounds

Background
Charlotte and Wilbur live in Zuckerman's barn. When Wilbur was going to be slaughtered, Charlotte devised a wonderful plan to save his life. She wove messages such as SOME PIG and TERRIFIC in her web, and people from miles around assumed that Wilbur had created them. When Mr. Zuckerman was awarded a special prize because Wilbur attracted so many people to the fair, Wilbur's future was assured—thanks to Charlotte.

Situation
Wilbur and Charlotte are alone after the award ceremony. Wilbur expresses his heartfelt gratitude to Charlotte for saving his life. He also expresses his joy at the prospect of their returning to the barn together. Charlotte breaks the news to Wilbur that she won't be going home and that in a day or two she'll be dead. Wilbur is distraught.

Comments
Wilbur is going to lose his best friend—the very spider who saved his life. Charlotte is totally resigned to the inevitability of her death and wants Wilbur to accepts its inevitability as well. Like many spiders which live in temperate regions, Charlotte cannot survive the cold. Her eggs however, will make it through the winter and hatch in the spring.

See index for other improvisations from this source.

Source: *Fly Away Home,* a screenplay by Robert Rodat and Vince McKewin, based on Bill Lishman's autobiography

Characters
One female, one male: Amy, twelve years old; Amy's father

Place
A hospital waiting room

Background
When Amy was three years old, her mother left home with her. Amy's mother had run out of patience with Amy's father's inability to earn a living. (He created strange works of art and useless inventions.) Amy did not see her father for the next nine years.

Situation
Amy and her mother were in a bad car accident, and both were hospitalized. Amy's father is called to the hospital to take Amy home. He must break the news that her mother did not survive.

Comments
Amy has bad memories of her father; she believes that he made her mother very unhappy. She doesn't want to live with him, but she doesn't have much choice. She has to deal with the trauma of losing her mother *and* going back to live in a place she doesn't like. Time has passed since father and daughter last saw each other, and they have both changed—emotionally and physically.

　　Amy's father is experiencing many conflicting feelings, perhaps regret and sorrow about his wife's death. He has undoubtedly missed Amy all these years and is happy to see her again. But now he will be responsible for Amy, and responsibility has never been his strong suit.

　　See index for other improvisations from this source.

Source: *Ira Sleeps Over,* a story by Bernard Waber (improvisation written by Maggie Nolan Donovan)

Characters
Two males: Ira; Reggie—young boys and best friends

Place
Reggie's bedroom

Background

Ira has been invited to spend the night next door at Reggie's house. He is very excited—this is his first sleepover—but he became anxious when his sister reminded him that he always sleeps with his teddy bear. All day long Ira agonized over whether to bring his teddy with him. His parents both told him to take his bear, but his sister kept teasing him, saying that Reggie will laugh and think he's a baby. When Ira and Reggie played together during the day, Ira kept bringing up teddy bears, but Reggie never responded. Finally, Ira decided to leave his bear at home.

Ira and Reggie played together all evening at Reggie's house. When Reggie's father announced that it was bedtime, the boys got into bed and Reggie began to tell a ghost story. Suddenly, he got up, went to his bureau drawer and pulled out a teddy bear. He got back into bed without comment.

Situation

Reggie and Ira are in twin beds in the dark. Ira begins to question Reggie about his bear and the dark. In the dialogue that follows, mostly Ira questioning and Reggie responding, each boy reveals his fears and his love for his teddy bear.

Comments

One thing that this dialogue reveals is that Reggie, like Ira, was afraid of ridicule because he slept with his bear. Reggie's concerns that day about the sleepover paralleled Ira's. These revelations are slow and hesitant and build on each other. After this conversation, Ira goes home and gets his teddy bear.

Source: *Justin and the Best Biscuits in the World,* a story by Mildred Pitts Walter

Characters

Two males: Justin, ten years old; Justin's grandfather

Place

Justin's house

Background

Justin feels frustrated; his mother and sisters are always demanding that he do this or do that. And no matter what he does, it's always the wrong thing. Justin's grandfather is coming to visit, and Justin has had to stay home to clean his messy bedroom. Justin *wanted* to make order out of the room's chaos, but he just wasn't equal to the task. He fell asleep with the room still a mess. His mother and sisters discovered what had happened and lectured him about not doing what he was told. Justin shouted back.

Situation
Grandpa comes in and asks the women to leave him alone with Justin. At first, Justin is still so upset that he can't speak. He tries not to cry, but when he begins to tell Grandpa about his unhappy life, he can't help himself. Grandpa listens and responds to Justin with understanding and empathy. Finally, Grandpa invites Justin for a visit to his ranch. Justin is absolutely delighted.

Comments
The improvisation can begin when Grandpa asks the women to leave or just after he does. The actor playing Justin must feel his sense of defeat and how it changes to elation when Grandpa offers him a way out. The bond the two feel is a deep and special one.

Source: *The Kid*, a film by Charlie Chaplin

Characters
Ensemble; Four males: A tramp; the kid, a six-year-old boy; two people from an orphanage

Place
The tramp's ramshackle house

Background
Six years ago a young woman, whose lover had deserted her, placed her baby in the back seat of an expensive car, hoping that a wealthy family would rescue the infant. However, the car was stolen, and the baby was abandoned on the street. A tramp found it, took it home, and raised it. The kid is now six years old.

The two of them have a scheme for earning money. The kid throws rocks at people's windows to break the glass, and the tramp comes by a few minutes later, selling new glass window panes. This is how they put food on the table.

One day, the kid became ill. A neighbor noticed and called the doctor, who was appalled by the squalid conditions the boy lived in. When he asked the tramp if the kid was his son, the tramp admitted to finding the boy as a baby. The tramp had carefully saved the note that the baby's mother had attached to his blanket, which reads: "Please take care of and love my baby." However, the doctor informed the state orphanage that the kid was living with the tramp illegally in unsatisfactory conditions.

Situation
Men from the orphanage arrive to take the kid away. The kid loves the tramp as his father; he calls him "papa." The tramp and the kid do everything they can to stay together.

Comments
A boy is being torn from his father. That the man is a tramp and not the kid's biological father makes his feelings no less acute. Of course, the people from the orphanage believe that they are doing what is right for the child's welfare. The actor playing the tramp should not attempt to imitate the famous Charlie Chaplin character. Today's equivalent of a tramp is a homeless person.

Source: *A Little Princess,* a musical play adapted by Susan Kosoff and Jane Staab, from the novel by Frances Hodgson Burnett

Characters
One male, one female: Captain Ralph Crewe; Sara, his young daughter

Place
The sitting room in Miss Minchin's Select Seminary for Girls in London, England; the late nineteenth century

Background
Captain Crewe, a widower, brought Sara from India, where they had always lived, to a boarding school in London. He and Sara adore each other. Although he has indulged her every whim, Captain Crewe believed the climate in India was not good for children and that Sara should be properly educated in London.

Situation
It is time for father and daughter to say good-bye. Neither one of them wants to be separated; they will miss each other desperately. Nonetheless, Captain Crewe believes he is doing what is best for his daughter. And Sara is resigned to abide by her father's wishes.

Comments
There is a deep sense of loss in this scene. The fact is that Captain Crewe and his daughter never see each other again. But that isn't what makes

them so sad here, although they may have a premonition that this parting is final. Each actor must play the conflict/subtext of not wanting to separate—while believing that it is the right thing to do.

See index for other improvisations from this source.

Source: *M Butterfly,* a play by David Henry Hwang

Characters
Ensemble; Two males, one female: Song Liling, four years old; his mother; his father; a teacher (optional)

Place
Outside the gates of the Peking Opera School, Peking, China

Background
Song Liling's father lost his land and his fortune. He could no longer support his large family and was forced to find other homes for several of his twelve children. Only his eldest daughter was of marrying age. After she left home, tradition stipulated that Song Liling, the youngest child, must leave home next. It was decided that he would attend the school that prepares boys for careers with the Peking Opera. This preparation is so rigorous, so all-encompassing, that students rarely see their families again once they enter the school.

Situation
Song Liling's mother and father are about to leave him at the gates of the school. This is their last moment together.

Comments
The actors must accept this long separation as a necessary event in their lives. Song Liling's parents love him—they simply cannot take care of him. Once he goes through those gates, they may never see him again. They know that the training will be stringent and sometimes cruel, but at least he will be given shelter, food, and a profession. Eventually, Song Liling becomes a Chinese opera star.

Source: *Meet the Austins,* a novel by Madeleine L'Engle

Characters
Two females: Vicky Austin, in her early teens; Maggie Hamilton, around ten years old

Place
Vicky's bedroom

Background
Several days ago, Maggie was orphaned when her single-parent father was killed in an airplane crash. He had been the copilot while Vicky's uncle was the pilot of the plane. Maggie has come to stay with the Austins for an indefinite amount of time. Vicky has learned that she must give Maggie her bed and move into her brother's room.

Situation
Maggie has just arrived in the Austins' home. She and Vicky meet for the first time.

Comments
Vicky's life has been happy up until now, but this stranger has disrupted everything and Vicky resents her. Deep down inside, Vicky may feel sorry for Maggie, but she finds it hard to empathize. Also, Maggie's plight brings up fears that something dreadful might happen to Vicky's parents. Maggie is not an easy child to like; she is very, very sad, angry, and anxious about her new life in this unfamiliar household.

Source: *The Secret Garden,* a novel by Frances Hodgson Burnett, adapted for the stage by Helen P. Avery

Characters
Ensemble; Two males, one female: Colin Craven, ten years old; Mr. Craven, Colin's father and master of Misselthwaite Manor; Mary Lennox, his niece, a girl about twelve years old

Place
Two locations at Misselthwaite Manor in Yorkshire, England—Colin's bedroom and the secret garden; early spring, 1910

Background
Colin's mother fell from a tree branch in her beloved garden when she was pregnant with Colin. Weakened by the fall, she died in childbirth. Colin's father, Mr. Craven, had the garden locked and the key buried. For many years, Colin has been kept in his room, away from his father, and treated like an invalid. Because his father is a hunchback, Colin is convinced that he, too, will grow a hump.

Young Mary Lennox is Mr. Craven's niece. Her parents recently died in India, so she was sent to live at Misselthwaite Manor. Hearing Colin's continual crying, Mary eventually discovered him in his room. She also discovered the door to the secret garden.

Situation

This improvisation is in two parts, in two different locales. The scene begins in Colin's bedroom where Mary tells the invalid that if he gets out of bed she will take him to the garden. Incredibly, he gets out of bed and goes with her. Mr. Craven, who has been traveling abroad, returns to find the children in the forbidden garden. He is amazed to see his son in normal physical condition.

Comments

This garden holds many memories for Mr. Craven. The branch from which his wife fell is still there. It is a shock to see his supposedly bedridden son up and about. The children have disobeyed him by entering the garden.

Mr. Craven has been living the life of a recluse these past years. Colin has mixed feelings about a father who virtually abandoned him and who (he believes) wants him dead. Colin knows very little about his mother, except that this garden was her favorite place.

Mary has recently lost her parents; finding the garden in which Colin's mother used to spend so much time will affect her as well.

The garden is an important aspect of this improvisation and should be clearly visualized; it has a special meaning for each character. The whole classroom can become the garden. Each student can imagine their own secret garden, move about in it, describe it, draw it, write about it.

A Note on *The Secret Garden*

This improvisation was done at the Florence Avenue Elementary School, an inner-city school in Los Angeles, in a class for aphasic students. These children are in third to sixth grade—ages eight to twelve. They have difficulties with language, so improvisations are done with few words. An hour was spent during which the whole classroom "became" the secret garden. Following this session, the children persuaded their mothers to rent the video version of *The Secret Garden*. They were very excited as they described the garden in the film, comparing it to their own secret gardens. One child checked out the book from the school library for the whole class to read. Because these children were personally involved with the story, they were motivated to rent the video and to read the book. They imagined this garden long before seeing someone else's interpretation of it. When they finally did see other people's versions of the garden, they had a greater appreciation of the story.

Source: *Slow Dance,* a UCLA student film by Carl Pfirman

Characters
Two males: Ben, a nine-year-old boy; Ben's father

Place
The living room of their home

Background
Ben's father was supposed to pick him up after baseball practice today, but he never showed up. Ben waited until it began to get dark; finally, he walked home by himself. When he arrived, there was no food in the house. He called his dad at work. His father apologized for forgetting Ben, adding that he would have to work late that night. Ben asked his father to pick up some grape jelly on the way home so that Ben could make a sandwich for dinner.

Situation
Ben's father arrives home late. He is drunk. He has forgotten the grape jelly. Ben tries to talk with him, but his father is not very coherent. To cheer him up, Ben puts on some music and dances with his father, who can barely stand. Finally, Ben helps his father to the couch, removes his shoes and tie, and covers him with a blanket.

Comments
You might think that this is an abusive home, even though Ben's father is not consciously abusive, he just seems to be overwhelmed with his own problems. Ben, who needs a parent, ends up being the parent. The only sign of Ben's mother is a family photograph in the living room.
    The following two situations, preceding the father's arrival, could be done as solo moments: Ben waiting for his father to pick him up at baseball practice, and Ben coming home to an empty house to find no food for dinner.

Source: *Stuart Little,* a novel by E.B. White

Characters
One male, one female: Stuart Little, a mouse; Margalo, a bird

Place
A garbage scow on New York City's East River

Background
Stuart Little was on his way to Central Park to try out his new ice skates, which his mother made from paper clips, when a dog began chasing him. Stuart found refuge in a garbage can and was still in it when two garbage collectors came to pick up the trash. They dumped the garbage and, unknowingly, Stuart onto the garbage scow at the East River. Stuart and the garbage were then headed out to sea.

Situation
Bravely, if unhappily, Stuart sits in the midst of garbage on the scow, preparing to meet his fate, when Margalo appears. She happened to see the garbage collectors take Stuart away, and she has come to rescue him.

Comments
The actors may choose any number of techniques to engineer the rescue—Margalo can drop a line and pull Stuart, Stuart can climb onto Margalo's back, and so forth. The focus for the actors should be on the emotions that Stuart and Margalo are feeling.

See index for other improvisations from this source.

Source: *Tales of a Fourth Grade Nothing,* a novel by Judy Blume

Characters
Ensemble; One female, two males (or any combination): Peter Warren Hatcher, a nine-year-old boy; Fudge, Peter's baby brother; Mrs. Hatcher, their mother

Place
The Hatchers' home

Background
Peter's biggest problem was his little brother, Fudge. Fudge was always in the way. He messed up everything he touched. When he got mad he would throw himself on the floor and scream and kick.

    Peter won a tiny green turtle at his friend's birthday party. Peter named his turtle Dribble. He is very fond of his new pet and takes good care of it.

Situation

The following situations involving Peter and Fudge should work well as improvisations.

Mrs. Hatcher cannot get Fudge to eat. One day Peter stands on his head, and Fudge eats. Now, every time his mother wants Fudge to eat, she tells Peter to stand on his head. Peter thinks the whole thing is ridiculous and doesn't want to do it anymore. His mother is frantic that Fudge will starve to death if Peter doesn't help her out.

One day, Mrs. Hatcher asks Sheila, the baby sitter, to watch Fudge at the playground. Peter and his friend persuade Sheila to play with them. Meanwhile, Fudge climbs to the top of the jungle gym and attempts to fly like a bird. He falls on his face and knocks his teeth out. He is rushed to the doctor. Mrs. Hatcher blames Peter for not looking after his baby brother, but Peter points out that it was Sheila's fault because she was the baby sitter. His mother does not see it his way.

The Hatchers bring Fudge to the movies, and he disappears under the seats. They are afraid he was kidnapped and frantically search under all the seats in the theater to find him. (Use the whole room or theatre for this improvisation as an exercise in looking for someone or something.)

Peter and two classmates put hours of work into a poster on city transportation. Fudge destroys it. Peter has to face his partners and tell them that all their hard work is down the drain.

Peter cannot find Dribble anywhere and asks Fudge if he has seen the turtle. Fudge tells Peter that he ate it. Peter tells Mrs. Hatcher, who is frantic that Fudge may die. Fudge is pleased with himself. Peter is filled with rage and sorrow over the untimely demise of his beloved pet.

Source: *Tom Sawyer,* a novel by Samuel L. Clemens (Mark Twain)

Characters

Ensemble; Five males: Tom Sawyer; Sid, his younger brother; Ben Rogers; Joe Harper; Huck Finn—each character is between the ages of ten and fourteen

Place

In front of Aunt Polly's house in a small village; mid-nineteenth century

Background

Tom Sawyer played hooky from school to go swimming with his pal, Huckleberry Finn. To punish him, Aunt Polly ordered him to whitewash the fence in front of her house.

Situation

Tom hates work. Yet, he absolutely must get the fence whitewashed before Aunt Polly comes home. So, he coerces his younger brother, as well as all his friends who wander by, to do his work for him, letting him off the hook.

Comments

Even if the actor playing Tom is familiar with the story of how Tom makes the work look like fun, he should use whatever means he chooses to get the others to fulfill his unspoken goal—to do the work that *he* is supposed to do. The other actors must find Tom's charm irresistible and have fun doing his work.

Source: *A Very Special Kwanzaa,* a book by Debbi Chocolate

Characters

Two males: Charlie Potter, a nine-year-old boy; Mr. Potter, his father; both are African American

Place

Charlie's bedroom

Background

Last year at the Kwanzaa festival Charlie was asked to stand in front of his class dressed in beads, a dashiki, and sandals, while his teacher, Ms. Marmelsteen, showed slides of Africa. When Ms. Marmelsteen left the room, Gilbert Crenshaw, the class bully, teased Charlie mercilessly.

Situation

This year the whole school will be celebrating Kwanzaa. Charlie has no desire to participate and fears he will once again be made to feel like a fool. His father finds Charlie in his bedroom, crying. Charlie tries to explain Gilbert's disdain for him and Kwanzaa. Mr. Potter is convinced that Charlie can ignore Gilbert and have a fine festival.

Comments

Charlie and his father have a warm and positive relationship, but each has a different take on the situation. Although Charlie goes along with what his father says, in his heart he believes that it is impossible to ignore someone like Gilbert. Once again, Charlie will be made to look like a fool.

Kwanzaa is a seven-day African American holiday created in 1966 by Maulana Karenga, a teacher who wanted to educate his people about their history. Celebrated from December 26 to January 1, the holiday is an attempt to bind the African harvest customs to the cultural and social history of African Americans. It is a time to celebrate kinship with family gatherings and reunions. From the East African Swahili phrase "matunde ya kwanza" (the first fruits), the word *kwanza* (first) was taken as the name of the holiday. The extra *a* was added to give the word seven letters. This represents the seven principles of Kwanzaa, one of which is stressed on each of the seven days. These are: unity, self-determination, collective work and responsibility, cooperative economics, purpose, creativity, and faith.

———➤◆≺———

5

Solo Moment

The nature and content of the situations in this chapter range from commonplace to the exotic. What unites and defines solo moments is their private nature. Not to be confused with Strasberg's "private moments"— scenes of intimacy (such as bathing oneself), instances of being "private in public" (Strasberg, 1965, 115)—solo moments occur when an actor is onstage alone. Whether or not they involve climactic developments in a scene or in a characters life, solo moments must always allow for a full and rich sense of the actor, as well as the situation at a specific point in time. In enacting solo moments, actors may or may not speak; indeed, they may not even discover, until in the moment, whether the nature of the scene evokes a verbal or nonverbal response.

Some people talk to themselves, others do not. Talking to oneself is usually involuntary; often people are not even aware that they are doing it. The same principle applies to the actor in the solo moment. Uta Hagen, in *A Challenge for the Actor* (1991), discusses the many reasons people have for talking to themselves. One is derived from the explanation of a psychologist, Dr. Palaci, who wrote that "the underlying reason for verbalizing when alone is a need to gain control over one's circumstances." People also talk to themselves to keep from forgetting something, to organize their thoughts, to prevent boredom, to express anger (by using expletives), and to solve a problem in the midst of a crisis.

Emotional preparation is of the utmost importance. The actor must fantasize, inventing everything that has happened up to this particular point in time. The actor must also resist the temptation to supply the audience with exposition. It is important to remember that when people talk to themselves, they know the scenario. Their verbalized comments are simply the random bubbles that arise from whatever is percolating underneath.

SOLO MOMENT SITUATIONS

One female

Addy's Surprise

Alice's Adventures in Wonderland

The Autobiography of My Mother

The Biggest Bear

The Blue Bird

A Blue-Eyed Daisy

Changes for Addy

Dollhouse

Fly Away Home

Happy Birthday Addy!

In Country

Journey Home

Journey to Topaz

The Kitchen God's Wife

Linda

Little Girl at the Fair

Meet Addy

Mirette on the High Wire

"The Old Chief Mshlanga"

"The Radish Cure"

The Rough-Face Girl

The Secret of Roan Inish

The Sound of a Miracle: A Child's Triumph Over Autism

The True Story of the Three Little Pigs

Tuck Everlasting

Uncle Tom's Cabin

Western Wind

One male

The Adventures of a Bear Called Paddington

Alexander and the Terrible, Horrible, No Good, Very Bad Day

Ali Baba and the Forty Thieves

The Biggest Bear

"The Bike"

The Blue Bird
"A Boy and His Dog"
"The Chicks"
"The Confession"
The Death
Escape From Slavery: The Boyhood of Frederick Douglass in His Own Words
"The Haircut"
"The Hero"
The Hunchback of Notre Dame
Jesus of 148th Street
Journey
"The Sirens"
The True Story of the Three Little Pigs

Source: *Addy's Surprise,* a novel by Connie Porter

Characters
One female: Addy Walker, a nine-year-old girl

Place
A church basement in Philadelphia, Pennsylvania; Christmas, the mid-nineteenth century

Background
Addy Walker and her mother escaped from slavery in North Carolina to freedom in Philadelphia. They are living in a garret above Mrs. Ford's shop, where Mrs. Walker works as a seamstress. Addy has never stopped dreaming of the day when she and her mother will be reunited with her father, her brother, and her sister, who are still living in slavery.

Situation
It is Christmas. Mrs. Walker and Addy have gone to church for services and dinner. After dinner, the children gather in darkness to watch a shadow play. Suddenly, the door opens and a figure appears in a shaft of light. It is Addy's father.

Comments
An actor can play Mr. Walker, or the character can be imagined by the actor playing Addy. The focus of the improvisation is Addy's reaction to seeing her father and to having her dream fulfilled. Surprise and great joy are doubtless at the forefront of Addy's feelings at this moment.

See also improvisations from the following sources: *Meet Addy, Addy Learns a Lesson, Happy Birthday Addy!, Addy Saves the Day*, and *Changes for Addy*.

Source: *The Adventures of a Bear Called Paddington,* a play adapted by Alfred Bradley, from the stories by Michael Bond

Characters
One male: Paddington, a bear

Place
The home of the Brown family at 32 Windsor Gardens, London, England

Background
The Browns met a bear at Paddington Railway Station and invited him to live with them and their two children, Judy and Jonathan. They named the bear Paddington after the place in which they found him.

Situation
An alarm clock rings. Paddington wakes up slowly, gets out of bed, goes downstairs backwards, and joins the family for breakfast. This is his first English breakfast, and the Brown family's first time having a bear to breakfast.

Comments
The actor playing Paddington should decide what he is going to have for breakfast before beginning this improvisation. It should be a rather elaborate meal. It is best if the bear does not use his hands. Members of the Brown family may or may not be present, but if they are, they should participate through their reactions to the difficulty Paddington is having with his breakfast.

Source: *Alexander and the Terrible, Horrible, No Good, Very Bad Day,* a book by Judith Viorst

Characters
One male or one female: A young boy or girl, aged four or older

Place
Anywhere

Background
Alexander had a terrible day. Everything went wrong—from getting up in the morning, to breakfast, to the ride to school, to school, to lunch, to going back to bed at night.

Situation
Describe a bad day you once had, or talk about the kinds of days you hate. What kinds of things happen to you on very bad days? Describe a good day.

Comments
This is like a "day in an actor's life" monologue. It can be used with actors of any age level. Use psychological gestures to demonstrate how you feel on bad days and good days. For an explanation of psychological gesture, see *To the Actor* by Michael Chekhov.

Source: *Ali Baba and the Forty Thieves,* a play by Wadeeha Atiyeh

Characters
One male: Ali Baba, an impoverished, peaceful woodcutter

Place
A robber's cave in Baghdad

Background
The time has come for Ali Baba to pay back the money he had borrowed from his pompous, rich brother. The kind and generous soul that he is, however, Ali Baba gave the money he saved to pay back the debt to someone who desperately needed it. His brother has made it clear that he will take Ali Baba's donkey if the debt is not paid by sundown. Ali Baba needs to find money to pay the debt; his livelihood depends on his donkey.

Situation
Ali Baba is sleeping under a tree in the desert. He wakes up to hear men approaching from a distance. Quickly, he hides. Robbers, following their chief and carrying bags full of jewels and gold, come into sight and stop in front of a large boulder. The chief raises his arm and cries "Open sesame!" A hidden door in the boulder swings open to reveal an enormous cavern full of treasures. Once they have deposited their cache, the chief exclaims, "Close sesame!" The door in the boulder swings shut. The robbers leave. Ali Baba must decide what to do with the knowledge of the treasure that has been revealed to him. He must decide whether to try to move the rock and, if he is able to move it, what he will do with the treasure, which he can put to important use.

Comments
The thrust of this solo moment is to physicalize Ali Baba's internal processes. Where he ends up is not as important as how he gets there.

Source: *Alice's Adventures in Wonderland,* a novel by Lewis Carroll

Characters
One female: Alice, a young girl

Place
Wonderland

Background
Alice was sitting with her sister on a river bank when she saw a white rabbit run by. He stopped, took a watch from his waistcoat pocket, looked at it, then popped down a nearby rabbit hole. Alice followed the rabbit into the hole and fell for miles and miles down what seemed to be a deep well. She landed, without getting hurt, in Wonderland.

Situation
Alice catches sight of the rabbit and chases after him. She finds herself in a long hall lined with doors. All of the doors are locked, and Alice becomes most distressed wondering how she will ever escape.

Comments
The actor playing Alice must accept the idea of following a rabbit down a hole to be a logical proposition. The feelings that motivate Alice's monologue should be believable and real.

See index for other improvisations from this source.

Source: *The Autobiography of My Mother,* a novel by Jamaica Kincaid

Characters
One female: Xuela, seven years old

Place
A river bank on the West Indian island of Dominica

Background
Xuela is the daughter of a Carib woman and a half-Scottish, half-African man. Her mother died the moment she was born. When Xuela was an infant, her father entrusted her to the care of his laundress. The woman had six children of her own, and they all seemed to be a burden. Xuela did not like the laundress and did not speak until she was four years old. Xuela yearned for her real mother: "I missed the face I had never seen."

Situation

Xuela is sitting on the river bank. She falls asleep and dreams about her mother. This is the first time she has seen her mother in a dream. She wakes up a different child.

Comments

In the novel, all Xuela sees in her dream are her mother's heels and the hem of her gown as she descends a ladder. Xuela longs to see more but cannot. However, the actor can see whatever images come; perhaps she'll see more than Xuela saw. Up to this point in her life, Xuela has never been loved by another human being; she longs to be loved. This dream of Xuela's mother is the child's first contact with this emotion.

Source: *The Biggest Bear*, a book by Lynd Ward

Characters

One male or one female: Johnny, between eight and ten years old; a bear, parents, neighbors (optional)

Place

Johnny's back yard in the country

Background

Johnny found an orphaned baby bear and raised him. Recently, the bear has gotten into a lot of trouble in the neighborhood—raiding kitchen shelves and corn fields, eating a neighbor's stash of bacon and hams, emptying all the sap buckets when the maple trees are being tapped in spring, eating all the apples in the orchard, and drinking the calves' milk. Now, he is not only full grown, but, because Johnny fed him so well, he is huge.

Situation

The neighbors complain to Johnny's father, who tells Johnny that it is time to send the bear back to the woods. Johnny must take his friend out to the woods and say good-bye.

Comments

This improvisation can be done in several ways. The neighbors and the father can be included in the scene, or this can be done as a solo moment for Johnny, saying good-bye to his friend. An imaginary bear, or an actor playing the bear, can be included. In Ward's story, the bear keeps returning until Johnny realizes the bear will have to be shot. He is about to do so when the bear runs into a trap and is taken to a zoo.

For other situations concerning a child's relationship with a pet, see also improvisations from the following sources: *Protecting Marie, Shiloh,* "A Boy and His Dog," "The Chicks," and *Fly Away Home.*

Source: "The Bike," an extract from the novel *A Summer Life* by Gary Soto

Characters
One male: Gary, the author, as a young boy

Place
A rural area; summertime

Background
Gary got his first bike and rode it around the block a few times, becoming bolder each time. He stopped when he saw a kid his age on a tricycle.

Situation
To prove how much bigger and bolder he is, Gary says to the kid, "You can run over my leg with your trike if you want." He stretches out on the sidewalk, and the kid runs over Gary's leg with his tricycle. As the tires roll over Gary's ankle, he feels pain. He is on the verge of tears when the kid asks if it hurts. Although he is nearly crying, Gary says no. After the kid has pedaled away, Gary lets his tears flow.

Comments
In Soto's novel, Gary rides his bicycle home with no fancy moves. A dog barks, which scares him and causes him to fall off the bike. He lies on the ground until his mother rescues him. If the actor chooses, these moments can be included in the improvisation. This is an exercise in making a transition; Gary starts out showing off, feeling like the king of the mountain, but he ends up with both his leg and his pride injured.

Source: *The Blue Bird,* a play by Maurice Maeterlinck

Characters
One male, one female: Tyltyl; Mytyl, his sister

Place
The Palace of Night

Background

Tyltyl and Mytyl have gone in search of the Blue Bird. They have searched the lands of Memory and the Future, and now they are in the Palace of Night. Night, in the form of an old woman, has warned them not to open the door of this palace; she told them that it is filled with unimaginable horrors. However, the children insisted that they must brave these perils in the hopes of finding the Blue Bird.

Situation

Tyltyl and Mytyl open the palace door and see beautiful gardens bathed in moonlight. Millions of fairy-like bluebirds fly among the moonbeams. The birds seem fearless. The children try to avoid hurting the bluebirds by catching them very gently. Suddenly, the birds begin to escape from the palace; with their hands full of struggling birds, Mytyl and Tyltyl run after them. But, once outside in the light, the birds fall dead.

Comments

This is a solo moment shared by the children. It can be done with one, or both characters, or with a whole class of students. A good amount of time should be devoted to visualizing the garden and the birds; the actors should be able to feel that they can reach out and touch them. The birds perish (as fish do when taken out of the water); they lose their color. It may be interesting to discuss why the birds died when they were removed from their natural habitat and why Night begged the children not to enter the palace. The actors should read the play for deeper understanding.

See index for other improvisations from this source.

Source: *A Blue-Eyed Daisy,* a novel by Cynthia Rylant

Characters

One female: Ellie, eleven years old

Place

Ellie's bedroom; late evening

Background

Tonight Ellie went to her first boy-girl party. Her older sisters spent a long time fixing her up for the big occasion, giving her an elegant hairdo and a manicure. Ellie wore a fancy dress made by her mother especially for the event. Nylons, patent leather shoes, and jewelry completed her outfit. Ellie was nervous about going to the party, and she felt rather foolish.

At the party, the guests played spin-the-bottle. When the bottle pointed at Ellie, a boy named Harold tried to kiss her, but she pulled away from him. Harold grabbed her again and kissed her on the mouth. This was her first kiss.

Situation

Ellie is now at home after the party; she is in her bedroom with the door closed. She is stretched out on her bed, and still wearing her new dress; she doesn't want to take it off yet. She can smell Harold's cologne on her hands. She is dizzy from the excitement of her first kiss.

Comments

This chapter in the novel is entitled "A Lovely Night," and indeed this is a lovely nocturnal moment for a girl (or boy). The actor may either remember her first kiss, or, if she has not yet experienced it, may imagine what it might be like. She will be aware of her special dress, hairdo, and accessories because they are all new and part of the experience. The sense of smell is important here; it is the lingering scent of Harold's cologne that enables Ellie to relive the moment of the kiss.

This exercise is reminiscent of Stanislavski's famous example of two young people who fall in love in a cucumber patch. Years later, neither of them can remember the person with whom they experienced their first love, but the smell of cucumbers enables them to vividly relive that moment.

See index for other improvisations from this source.

Source: "A Boy and His Dog," a short story by Martha Brooks, in *Who Do You Think You Are?: Stories of Friends and Enemies,* a collection selected by Hazel Rochman and Darlene Z. McCampbell

Characters

One male: Buddy, a young boy

Place

Buddy's bedroom

Background

Buddy has an old dog named Alphonse. Because Alphonse had not been feeling well, Buddy took him to the veterinarian. The vet diagnosed cancer. Buddy took Alphonse home.

Situation

This is Buddy's last night with Alphonse. His mother offers him a sleeping pill, which he refuses. Alphonse is in Buddy's bed. Buddy decides to tell his dog what he plans to do with his life, in as much detail as possible, so that the dog will know everything about Buddy before it dies.

Comments
Buddy loves his dog very much; the way he gets through the night is to keep talking to Alphonse. It is an interesting exercise to think about the rest of your life when you're just a young boy. An improvisation also could be done using the scene between Buddy and the veterinarian.

For other situations concerning a child's relationship with a pet, see also improvisations from the following sources: *Protecting Marie, Shiloh, The Biggest Bear,* "The Chicks," and *Fly Away Home.*

Source: *Changes for Addy,* a novel by Connie Porter

Characters
One female: Addy Walker, a ten-year-old girl

Place
Trinity American Methodist Episcopal Church in Philadelphia, Pennsylvania; the mid-nineteenth century

Background
Although the Civil War was over, Addy's family still had not been reunited. One day the Walkers received a letter informing them that Addy's baby sister, Esther, and her Aunt Lula and Uncle Solomon, were on their way to Philadelphia. Addy and her brother Sam searched the city until Addy found Aunt Lula and baby Esther—only to discover that Uncle Solomon had died en route. Ill and exhausted from the journey, Aunt Lula died a short time later. Addy is grief-stricken.

Situation
Addy has been asked to read the Emancipation Proclamation at the church's emancipation celebration. Addy feels heartsick at the cost of freedom—Solomon and Lula's deaths and the time lost with Esther. She is not sure that she can read the words about freedom. Her mother helps her dare to try. Addy walks to the front of the church, opens the scroll, looks out at the congregation, and reads the famous statement.

Comments

The words read by the actor playing Addy are those that forever changed the lives of all the people Addy loves. She has been chosen to read them because she is a strong, expressive reader. Still, underneath the import of the words and her pride at being chosen to read them is her deep sadness that comes from learning the price freedom has cost her family. The Emancipation Proclamation is available at most libraries.

See also improvisations from the following sources: *Meet Addy*, *Addy Learns a Lesson*, *Addy's Surprise*, *Happy Birthday Addy!*, and *Addy Saves the Day*.

Source: "The Chicks," an extract from the novel *A Summer Life* by Gary Soto

Characters
One male: Gary, the author, as a young boy

Place
Gary's backyard in the country; summertime

Background
Gary's family kept chickens, and Henrietta was Gary's favorite chicken. One day, a cat attacked Henrietta, hurting her badly. Gary's brother, Rick, told him that Henrietta would have to be killed; she was too injured to live. Gary couldn't do it, so Rick did it for him.

Situation
Gary scoops up Henrietta's body with a shovel and buries her next to Willy, another chicken.

Comments
Gary feels responsible for Henrietta's death; he should have kept an eye out for the cat. Henrietta was not just a chicken, she was his beloved pet.
For other situations concerning a child's relationship with a pet, see also improvisations from the following sources: *Protecting Marie*, *Shiloh*, *The Biggest Bear*, "A Boy and His Dog," and *Fly Away Home*.

Source: "The Confession," an extract from the novel *A Summer Life* by Gary Soto

Characters
One male: Gary, the author, as a young child

Place
The confessional in a Catholic church

Background
Gary is a Catholic and is required to confess his sins to a priest once a week.

Situation
Gary confesses.

Comments
The actor can draw on personal experience or his imagination to supply the content of the confession; it is preferable that the actor use an actual incident. All children do things that are "wrong," and although the sins may not amount to much, the Catholic religion requires that they be confessed. The sin might be something simple, such as, "I stole an apple from Tommy's lunch box." Because acting is, in essence, confessing something about yourself, this is a good exercise for the student. If the idea of confessing to a priest is too difficult or too strange, the actor can confess to the class or to a friend.

Source: *The Death*, an incident from real life, as told to Sandra Caruso by an anonymous source

Characters
One male: A boy, four years old

Place
His father's bedroom; early morning

Background
The boy's father has been ill for a long time. Every day after school the boy would visit his father in his bedroom.

Situation
One morning the boy goes to his father's bedroom and finds that the father's bed is stripped. Also, most of his father's belongings have been removed from the room. His mother is nowhere to be found.

Comments
The boy's mother never speaks with him about his father's death. She is unable to cope with the loss of her husband, and, therefore, she cannot help her child. Then she disappears. The boy loses two parents at the same time. He ends up in a mental institution.

This is a frightening situation. The teacher might be advised to follow up with a discussion as to how the mother (or other adult) might have handled it in a more sensitive fashion. This would be a good improvisation to do for a parents group, to stimulate discussion. In the actual incident, the boy was only four years old.

Source: *Dollhouse*, a UCLA student film by Nicole Halpin

Characters
One female: A little girl, approximately eight years old

Place
The living room of an apartment

Background
The little girl's parents have separated; she and her very depressed mother are moving out of their apartment. They are alone, with no relatives or friends nearby.

Situation
The furniture is covered with white sheets. This is the child's last look at the home in which she has lived all of her life.

Comments
In this short, silent film, there is no reference to what may have transpired between the parents. The actor must fill in the family history. What are the memories in this room? Did she hear her parents fighting? Were there happy moments?

In the film, her mother bought a dollhouse for the little girl to cheer her up and placed it in the middle of the empty living room of their new apartment. This improvisation might be extended to include the little girl's arrival in her new home.

Source: *Escape From Slavery: The Boyhood of Frederick Douglass in His Own Words*, memoirs by Frederick Douglass, edited by Michael McCurdy

Characters
One male: Frederick Douglass, a six-year-old boy

Place
The home of a plantation owner in Talbot County, Maryland; 1823

Background

Frederick Douglass was born a slave in 1817. When he was young he lived with many members of his immediate and extended family in a cabin on one of the master's plantation farms. These early childhood years were happy ones for Frederick. He played in the woods and creek near the cabin. He lived in a loving, if crowded, environment.

Situation

Frederick is six years old. One day Frederick's grandmother takes him for a long walk to the plantation owner's house. And then she leaves—without telling Frederick that she was leaving or that he must now live in his owner's house. He discovers what happens when another child blurts out that Frederick's grandmother has abandoned him.

Comments

The actor playing Frederick can react in many ways, with or without words. However, the momentous realization must permeate whatever he does. Remember: Frederick was totally unprepared for what has happened. He will experience any number of feelings—shock, abandonment, grief, anger, fear. The improvisation can begin with the child telling Frederick that his grandmother has left, or it can begin immediately after Frederick has heard the news.

See also the following improvisations.

Source: *Escape From Slavery: The Boyhood of Frederick Douglass in His Own Words*, memoirs by Frederick Douglass, edited by Michael McCurdy

Characters

One male: Frederick Douglass, eight years old

Place

A boat sailing toward Baltimore, Maryland; the early nineteenth century

Background

Frederick has been told that he will be sent to Baltimore to live with Hugh and Sophia Auld and their son, Thomas. Frederick washed himself in the creek before donning his first long pants and "tuck-in" shirt for the journey.

Situation

Frederick is on board a boat bound for Baltimore—with a flock of sheep destined for slaughter as his traveling companions. As the boat sets sail, he looks one last time at the plantation where he has spent the previous two years of his life.

Comments

Frederick is glad to leave the plantation house and believes that, no matter where he ends up, it can't be any worse than where he has been and what he has endured. The actor must clearly imagine the plantation. For Frederick, it is the repository of many, many memories. He may or may not choose to speak.

See also the following improvisation.

Source: *Escape From Slavery: The Boyhood of Frederick Douglass in His Own Words,* memoirs by Frederick Douglass, edited by Michael McCurdy

Characters
One male: Frederick Douglass, eight years old

Place
A house on Alliciana Street in Baltimore, Maryland; 1825

Background
Frederick has been sent from his home on his master's plantation to live in Hugh and Sophia Auld's home in Baltimore. He made the journey aboard a boat, a flock of sheep his only traveling companions.

Situation
Frederick goes to the door of the Auld's home. He has no idea what kind of people they will be. He knows they are white, and he has never been treated kindly by any white person. He also knows that this is where he must live no matter what. He has no choice.

Comments
The actor may or may not verbalize his feelings throughout this scene. It is important that the actor convey his overwhelming apprehension, as well as a deep sense of resignation.

See also the preceding improvisations.

Source: *Fly Away Home*, a screenplay by Robert Rodat and Vince McKewin, based on Bill Lishman's autobiography

Characters
One female: Amy, twelve years old

Place
Amy's bedroom in her father's house in rural Canada

Background
When Amy was three years old her mother left home, taking Amy with her. She had no more patience with Amy's father's inability to earn a living. (He created strange works of art and useless inventions.) Amy had no contact with her father for nine years. When Amy's mother was killed in a car accident, Amy's father was called to the hospital to take his daughter home.

Situation
Amy's father shows her into her old bedroom, which he has used as a storage room. He promises to clean it up. Amy has some vague memories of this room. Her father leaves her alone.

Comments
Amy's life has been tragically disrupted. Her mother is dead, and her father is like a stranger. Her room has been abandoned all these years. Another actor, playing the father, could bring Amy into the room. The actor playing Amy should be specific about the objects in the room and the memories and emotions they conjure up.

See also the preceding improvisations.

Source: *Fly Away Home,* a screenplay by Robert Rodat and Vince McKewin, based on Bill Lishman's autobiography

Characters
One female: Amy, twelve years old

Place
The woods near Amy's home in rural Canada

Background
When Amy was three years old, her mother left home, taking Amy with her. She had no more patience with Amy's father's inability to earn a liv-

ing. (He created strange works of art and useless inventions.) Amy had no contact with her father for nine years. When her mother was killed in a car accident, Amy began living with her father again in her old home. She is very unhappy with her life.

Situation
On this particular day, Amy refuses to go to school. Developers have been clearing trees near her home. Amy goes into the freshly plowed area and discovers a nest of abandoned goose eggs. She takes the eggs home.

Comments
The baby geese have lost their mother, just as Amy has. She keeps the eggs at home until they hatch. Let this situation inspire an improvisation between Amy and her father and the conflict that arises when the whole house is filled with baby geese.

For other situations concerning a child's relationship with a pet, see also improvisations from the following sources: *Protecting Marie*, *Shiloh*, *The Biggest Bear*, "A Boy and His Dog," and "The Chicks."

Source: "The Haircut," an extract from the novel *A Summer Life* by Gary Soto

Characters
One male: Gary, the author, as a young boy

Place
Gary's bedroom in a house in the country; summertime

Background
Rhinehardt, Gary's twelve-year-old friend, cut Gary's hair. The result is hideous to behold.

Situation
Gary looks in the mirror. He is horrified—and furious with Rhinehardt.

Comments
The actor must visualize that haircut—bare spots, patches of long hair, and so on. A bad haircut can be traumatizing. It's especially painful when you're young and vulnerable to the taunts of other children. Hair doesn't grow back overnight.

Source: *Happy Birthday Addy!*, a novel by Connie Porter

Characters
One female: Addy Walker, a nine-year-old black girl

Place
A boarding house in Philadelphia, Pennsylvania; the mid-nineteenth century

Background
Addy and her parents escaped from slavery in North Carolina and are living as free people in Philadelphia. Although their lives are far better now, the Walkers must contend with a great deal of prejudice. And they dearly miss Addy's brother and sister, who are still enslaved.

While Addy was a slave, her birthday was never observed. To help raise Addy's spirits and to restore something slavery had denied her, an older and wiser friend, who lives in the boarding house, has encouraged Addy to choose a special day as her birthday.

Situation
Addy is awakened from a sound sleep by a great hubbub in the street outside her window. She hears the explosion of cannon balls, gun shots, people cheering, whistles blowing, and church bells ringing. Addy jumps out of bed to investigate and discovers that the uproar is in response to momentous news: the Civil War is over. In the midst of the excitement, Addy chooses this very day, April 9th, as her birthday.

Comments
The actor playing Addy will show the joy and excitement created by the end of the war. However, the deeper feeling is about the end of slavery and the hope generated that her family will be reunited. Addy's parents may or may not be a part of the scene.

See also improvisations from the following sources: *Meet Addy, Addy Learns a Lesson, Addy's Surprise, Addy Saves the Day,* and *Changes for Addy.*

Source: "The Hero," an extract from the novel *A Summer Life* by Gary Soto

Characters
One male: Gary, the author, as a young boy

Place
The backyard of a house in the country; summertime

Background
Tony was Gary's best friend; they told each other everything. Tony once told Gary that he would die for the president. From that time on, Gary thought of him as a hero. However, one day Tony moved away and left without saying good-bye.

Situation
Gary goes to Tony's vacant house and peeks in a window.

Comments
What Gary sees inside is left to the actor's imagination. What did the family leave behind? What are Gary's memories of Tony? Are some of Tony's belongings still there? Maybe there is something Gary gave him that he left behind.

Source: *The Hunchback of Notre Dame,* a Walt Disney movie by Gary Trousdale and Kirk Wise, based on the novel *Notre-Dame de Paris* by Victor Hugo, screenplay by Irene Mecchi, Tab Murphy, Jonathan Roberts, Bob Tzudiker, and Nona White

Characters
One male: Quasimodo, a young man

Place
Paris, France

Background
Quasimodo was abandoned as a poor infant on the steps of the Cathedral of Notre Dame. He has lived his entire life in the cathedral's bell tower. He knows nothing, except for what he has observed, about the world below. Usually Quasimodo watches the annual Festival of Fools with his friends the gargoyles. However, this year, they persuaded Quasimodo to attend the festival himself. Quasimodo dresses in a disguise and joins the parade of people wearing costumes, musicians playing music, and peasants dancing.

Situation
The time comes for the crowning of the King of Fools, who is chosen for having the ugliest face in Paris. Each contender's grotesque mask is removed, until Quasimodo is reached. He is not wearing a mask and is declared the ugliest King of Fools ever.

Comments

The actor playing Quasimodo must feel the terror, shame, and rejection such an experience would cause. This is his first venture out into the world, and it is even worse then he could have imagined. It might be helpful for the actor to imagine himself surrounded by a jeering crowd. In the movie, Quasimodo begs for help, which is finally delivered by a young woman, but the situation can be resolved in any way that seems honest and real.

Source: *In Country,* a film by Norman Jewison, based on Bobbie Ann Mason's novel of the same name

Characters
One female: A young woman

Place
The Vietnam Veterans' Memorial, Washington, District of Columbia

Background
This young woman's father died in Vietnam before she was born. She was raised by her mother; the two of them have had a difficult time.

Situation
The young woman visits the Vietnam Memorial and touches her father's name, which is carved in the granite. This is the closest she's ever come to him.

Comments
The actor can create whatever back story she desires in terms of her relationship with her mother: what it has been like growing up without a father, what her mother has told her about her father, her own fantasies. This improvisation also can be done with the entire class, using the walls of the room. Actors should know exactly which name they're looking for and what they are feeling; they should also have an awareness of the other people at the memorial wall. When done in total silence, the scene can be quite moving.

Source: *Jesus of 148th Street,* a UCLA student film by Timothy Martin Mills

Characters
One male: A ten-year-old boy

Place
148th Street in any large city

Background
A little boy saw a photo in a tabloid newspaper with the headline, "Black Jesus Seen on 148th Street." He went looking for this man.

Situation
After a long search, the little boy spots a homeless person with long hair who looks like the man in the newspaper photo. The little boy goes running after him, believing him to be Jesus.

Comments
This situation could be extended into a two-person improvisation, in which the little boy and the homeless man interact. The film ends with the little boy running toward the homeless man, who has stopped to wait for him. Jesus must have a particular meaning for the actor playing the little boy.

Source: *Journey*, a novel by Patricia MacLachlan

Characters
One male: Journey, an eleven-year-old boy

Place
A bedroom in his grandparents' house

Background
Journey's mother walked out one day, leaving Journey and his sister to live with their grandparents. Journey pressured his grandfather to show him family pictures. Grandfather reluctantly revealed that Journey's mother had torn up some baby pictures of the two children.

Situation
Since the day that Journey's mother left, no one has entered her room. One day, Bloom, Journey's pet cat, runs into the room and jumps into a box under the bed. When Journey attempts to pull Bloom out of the box, he finds that it is filled with the torn photographs. He attempts to put the pieces of the puzzle together.

Comments
Use actual torn pictures for this improvisation. Later on in the story, Journey pastes the pieces together: this would be an interesting exercise for the actor. If he grasps the significance of putting these pieces together it should be exciting. Journey may never have actually seen his father—imagine the thrill of watching his father emerge from so many torn bits of

paper. These memories and discoveries may cause happiness, sadness, or a mixture of both.

See also index for other improvisations from this source.

Source: *Journey to Topaz*, a novel by Yoshiko Uchida

Characters
One female: Yuki, ten years old

Place
On a train bound for Utah from California; during World War II, at dusk

Background
Yuki, her family, and other Japanese-Americans are being transported from a holding camp in San Francisco to an internment camp somewhere in the Utah desert.

Situation
As the train leaves San Francisco, Yuki looks back and sees the San Francisco Bay and the bridge with the lights along it. This revives Yuki's memories of home. Everyone on the train is silent. Suddenly, a voice breaks the spell: "Shades down."

Comments
This is the first time in four months that Yuki has seen anything other than the filthy stables at the holding camp. This moment is both stimulating and frightening. Yuki experiences the excitement of seeing the bridge and the world, but she also realizes that she is leaving California, her home. And the future is unknown.

See also the following improvisation. See improvisation from the following source: *Journey Home.*

Source: *Journey to Topaz*, a novel by Yoshiko Uchida

Characters
One female: Yuki, twelve years old

Place
The Vase: Yuki's home in Berkley, California; World War II; and The Letter: the internment camp in the Utah desert; World War II

Situation
These are two solo moments to be improvised with an object.

The Vase
When the family was evacuated, Yuki's mother had wrapped her best crystal bud vase in a gray wool sweater and carried it with her from Berkeley to the desert. It is a special vase, which her mother placed beside the photographs of Yuki's grandparents on the anniversary of their deaths. It was also used to commemorate Yuki's younger sister, who died when she was a baby.

The day before Yuki's family is to leave Berkeley for the internment camp, Yuki is washing the vase. She drops it by accident and it falls to the floor, breaking into many pieces. Yuki feels terrible. She knows how much the vase means to her mother. Yuki also believes the smashed vase signifies that something terrible has happened to her brother, Ken, who is away fighting for the United States Army. She sweeps up the broken glass with this dreadful thought in mind.

The Letter
Yuki receives an official letter from the army regarding her older brother, Ken. She is terrified that it may be a notification of his death, so she is greatly relieved when she reads that he only has been wounded. He is in a hospital recovering from a leg wound. When he is discharged from the hospital he will be sent home.

Comments
We become very attached to objects, and we endow them with emotional qualities. The handling of objects is an important aspect of the actor's technique. In this improvisation, these two objects, the vase and the letter, are of great importance to Yuki.

See improvisation from the following source: *Journey Home.*

Source: *Journey Home,* a novel by Yoshiko Uchida

Characters
One female: Yuki, twelve years old

Place
An automobile, driving down a street in Berkeley, California, 1945; just after the end of World War II

Background
Yuki and her family, along with thousands of other Japanese-Americans,

are returning from internment camps in Utah, where they have been detained for two years.

Situation

Yuki and her family drive by their former home. It is now occupied by strangers. Yuki's dog died while she was in the internment camp, and she looks at the front porch where they used to sit. She notices that the camellias aren't blooming.

Comments

There are many more details that Yuki would notice in seeing the home where she spent the first ten years of her life. The actor playing Yuki should be aware of the many mixed emotions involved: nostalgia, anger at not being able to return, sadness, longing, fear of the future. The family has no idea where they will live now. They must start all over again.

See improvisation from the following source: *Journey to Topaz.*

Source: *The Kitchen God's Wife,* a novel by Amy Tan

Characters

One female, ensemble: A young girl, between five and ten years old; any number of servants

Place

The kitchen table of the girl's home in China; the 1950s

Background

The girl's mother took her out for a wonderful day, during which they did all kinds of special things. They went to places where the best things in the world could be found; they bought real leather shoes, ice cream, books, and they went to the movies. Then they came home for a simple meal. The girl watched her mother comb her long black hair at her dressing table. The mother showed her some embroidery stitches. She took out all her jewelry, telling her daughter that someday it would be hers and that when she put it on people will think she's worth something. They climbed into bed together, and her mother sang her to sleep.

Situation

It is the following morning. The daughter awakens to find her mother no longer in bed beside her. She opens her bedroom door and looks out. Servants pass by, carrying chamber pots. One servant comes in with two steaming bowls of "syen do jang," a salty-tasting soy milk soup. The girl asks for her mother. The servant's only answer is: "Eat the soup quickly, before it gets cold," but the girl is not hungry. Eventually, the servant returns for the bowl, takes it, and leaves. Nobody seems to know where her mother is—or else they're not telling. Suddenly, someone bursts into the room with the mother's hair held in one hand, like a horse's tail.

Comments

This situation is solely from the point of view of the little girl. None of the adults are aware of what she is going through. A little girl loses her mother, but nobody will tell her anything. She never does see her mother again. Later, an aunt finally reveals where her mother is buried. Her mother probably took her own life.

This is basically a solo moment, but the actor needs the scurrying of the adults to emphasize the feeling of loneliness.

Source: *Linda*, a UCLA student film by Vivian Weisman

Characters
One female: Linda, an eleven-year-old girl

Place
A hallway outside the living room of Linda's home; early morning

Background
Linda goes to a Catholic school, but she is frightened by some of the nuns and would prefer to stay home. She often feigns illness in the morning to get out of going to school, but her mother sends her anyway. Her mother is preoccupied with a boyfriend.

Situation
Linda overhears her mother telling her boyfriend that Linda is too much trouble. She is thinking of sending Linda away to school in Switzerland.

Comments
Linda is a lonely little girl, without a father and with an unhappy mother. The boyfriend is the center of her mother's attention. Feigning illness is one way for Linda to get her mother's attention. To be sent away to school is a frightening prospect, because Linda would then be even farther away from her mother.

Source: *Little Girl at the Fair,* an incident from real life, as observed by Sandra Caruso at the Martha's Vineyard Agricultural Fair, 1997

Characters
One female: A five-year-old girl

Place
A country fair

Background
The little girl is at the fair with her mother. Somehow, the two of them are separated.

Situation
The girl, who is carrying a stuffed animal, suddenly realizes that her mother is gone.

Comments
In the original incident, the child became hysterical and began throwing her toy animal around. However, there are other reactions that a child might have in this situation, and the actor need not feel compelled to follow the original. In the author's observation, the child seemed to be displaying an inordinate amount of anger. When the mother was finally found, she didn't seem very concerned. The mother's attitude may have some bearing on the child's reaction.

Source: *Meet Addy,* a novel by Connie Porter

Characters
One female: Addy Walker, a nine-year-old slave girl; Confederate Army soldiers (optional)

Place
A Confederate Army camp in North Carolina; 1864

Background
Addy and her mother despaired that the Civil War—which promised to end their lives of slavery—would never be over. In desperation, they escaped from the plantation and began the long trek to Philadelphia and freedom disguised as a man and a boy. They traveled by night and slept by day, encountering danger and hardship along the way. At long last,

they came upon a certain set of train tracks, which meant that a safe house could be found nearby.

Situation
A train passes by and Addy follows it along the track, leaving her mother behind. She unexpectedly stumbles into a campground full of Confederate soldiers. By the time she realizes where she is, it's too late to retreat. Her mother cannot rescue her. Addy must figure out how to escape.

Comments
In the book, Addy realizes that the soldiers think she is one of the camp children and take her presence for granted. The challenge for the actor is to feel Addy's internal panic at the prospect of being discovered, while maintaining an outward calm to avoid arousing suspicion. Once Addy realizes where she is and the danger she faces, she must quickly determine a way out of the predicament. Actors playing the soldiers may help make the situation work.

See also improvisations from the following sources: *Addy Learns a Lesson, Addy's Surprise, Happy Birthday Addy!, Addy Saves the Day,* and *Changes for Addy.*

Source: *Mirette on the High Wire,* a story by Elizabeth Arnold McCully (improvisation written by Maggie Nolan Donovan)

Characters
One female: Mirette, a young girl

Place
A small, enclosed courtyard in Paris, France; the late 1800s

Background
Mirette's widowed mother runs a boarding house for actors, musicians, and other performers who are passing through Paris. Lately, a mysterious stranger has taken up residence; when he arrived, he requested a private room at the back of the house and said he would take his meals alone in his room.

One day Mirette looked out into the courtyard and saw the stranger walking along the clothesline. Fascinated, she begged him to teach her how to walk the tightrope. He refused. Mirette was disappointed but undeterred: she decided to teach herself. She had fallen in love with the high wire and knew that nothing but learning to walk it would make her happy. Mirette practiced for many days on a low wire and had countless falls.

Situation
Mirette is alone in the courtyard. Her obsession with the wire is her secret. She begins to practice and falls again and again. Finally, she succeeds in crossing the wire from end to end.

Comments
Mirette's determination and concentration are complete. Although her falls must hurt, she ignores the pain, and perseveres. She is not afraid. This improvisation could include words but might be more powerful as pure movement. The scene is less about physical dexterity than it is about revealing the character of Mirette. However, the actor must make the fall real; perhaps using a piece of string or a floor board to walk on.

See index for other improvisations from this source.

Source: "The Old Chief Mshlanga," a short story by Doris Lessing, in *Somehow Tenderness Survives: Stories of Southern Africa*, selected by Hazel Rochman

Characters
One female: A girl, about ten years old, the daughter of Nkosis Jordan

Place
South Africa, the deserted village of Chief Mshlanga and his people; the 1980s

Background
The Jordans have heard that Chief Mshlanga and his people were moved two hundred miles east, to a native reserve, and that their land will be opened up for white settlement.

Situation
The little girl goes to visit the village again. It is empty and desolate. There are few reminders of the huts—pieces of thatched roof, some planting gone wild.

Comments
It is for the actor to imagine what the village was like before and what it is like now, to experience the deep sense of loss.

Source: "The Radish Cure," a story by Betty MacDonald, in *Mrs. Piggle-Wiggle*

Characters
Two females: Patsy, a young girl; Patsy's mother

Place
Patsy's bedroom

Background
Mrs. Piggle-Wiggle is very small, smells like cookies, and has a lump of magic on her back. She lives in an upside-down house. All of the children in town adore her. And, since Mrs. Piggle-Wiggle has the magical power to cure children of bad behavior, all of the grown-ups love her too.

Patsy developed an aversion to bathing. Desperate, her mother called Mrs. Piggle-Wiggle for a cure. Mrs. Piggle-Wiggle suggested that she have Patsy give up washing until she was covered with about half an inch of dirt. Then, her mother was to plant radish seeds in the rich loam covering Patsy's body.

Situation
One morning, several weeks later, Patsy wakes up to find herself covered with a lush growth of little green leaves.
Comments
The actor playing Patsy should take the time to discover all of the green leaves and to react to the situation. She may or may not choose to speak. In MacDonald's story, Patsy's mother starts pulling out the radishes for Patsy. The actor does not have to resolve the situation by taking a bath, but it is Mrs. Piggle-Wiggle's intended cure.

See also the improvisation from "The Answer Backer Cure."

Source: *The Rough-Face Girl,* an Algonquin Indian Cinderella story as told by Rafe Martin

Characters
One female: The Rough-Face Girl

Place
A village on the shores of Lake Ontario

Background

For many years, the youngest daughter of a poor man was forced to do all the work of the household by her two elder sisters. They mocked and tormented her constantly, calling her the Rough-Face Girl. (Sparks from the fire, which it was one of her duties to tend, had left her entire body burned and scarred.)

Her sisters had set their sights on marrying the Invisible Being, a great and powerful man who lived with his sister in the biggest wigwam in the village. However, to all women but his future bride, he was invisible; although the sisters claimed they had seen him, they were unable to prove the truth of their assertion and were sent away humiliated.

The Rough-Face Girl *has* seen the Invisible Being and was able to answer correctly his sister's questions. Clearly, she was the Invisible Being's intended bride.

Situation

The Rough-Face Girl is preparing for her wedding to the Invisible Being by bathing in Lake Ontario. As she washes herself, she becomes beautiful—her scars disappear, her skin becomes smooth, and her hair grows long and glossy.

Comments

The actor should feel the water slowly allowing the beauty that is inside the Rough-Face Girl to show on the outside. It is preferable not to use words or even much physical action to reveal the transformation that is at the heart of this improvisation.

See also improvisations from the following sources: *Cinderella in China*, *The Native American Cinderella*, and *The Russian Cinderella*.

Source: *The Secret of Roan Inish,* a film by John Sayles, based on the book *The Secret of Roan Inish* by Rosalie K. Fry

Characters

One female: Fiona Coneelly, a ten-year-old girl

Place

The isolated island of Roan Inish off the west coast of Ireland; just after World War II

Background

Fiona's family now lives on the mainland, but they used to live on Roan Inish. Poverty and loneliness drove everyone from the island; the seals are now its only inhabitants. When her mother died, Fiona was sent to live with her grandparents. It was her grandfather who told her the story of the loss of her baby brother, Jamie. During the move from the island three years ago, Jamie floated out to sea in his cradle and was never seen again.

Situation

Fiona, her grandfather, and a young boy row out to Roan Inish to fish. While her grandfather and the boy are fishing, Fiona wanders into the house in which her family once lived. She notices hot ashes on the floor, the remnants of a recently built fire in a supposedly abandoned cottage. There are also broken shells, an indication that someone has been eating seafood. As she runs out of the house, she sees a naked little boy fleeing from her. She realizes it's Jamie, her brother—he has survived! He has been living alone on this island with only the seals to watch over him. Fiona calls after him, but he runs away terrified; he has never seen a human being before.

Comments

This scene requires a great deal of imagination on the part of the actor playing Fiona. She must visualize the house, with its dirt floor, stucco walls, and grass roof; it has the atmosphere of an abandoned house festooned with cobwebs. She must also picture Jamie, who must look very strange because he's been living like a wild animal. She has made an extraordinary discovery—Jamie was not drowned at sea three years ago. He's alive.

See index for other improvisations from this source.

Source: "The Sirens," an extract from the novel *A Summer Life* by Gary Soto

Characters

One male: Gary, the author, as a five-year-old boy

Place

The backyard of Gary's house in the country; summertime

Background

Gary was playing outside when he heard sirens. He asked his brother what they meant. His brother said that they were air raid sirens, announcing that war had been declared.

Situation

Gary is playing with ants in the dirt when he hears the sirens again. The noise seems to make the ants angry. An ant bites Gary, and he kills it. At that moment, he realizes that squashing an ant is like dropping a bomb from an airplane. He tries to revive the ant, but it is too late.

Comments

This is a poignant foreshadowing of war. It is impressive that a five-year-old boy has such a comprehension of what war is. His size in relation to the ants is similar to that of an airplane bomber to the boy. The actor is dealing with the senses of sound, sight, and touch.

Source: *The Sound of a Miracle: A Child's Triumph Over Autism*, a novel by Annabel Stehli

Characters

One female: Georgie, eleven years old

Place

The front yard of Georgie's house

Background

Georgie has been diagnosed as autistic, a developmental disability that typically appears during the first three years of life. Caused by a neurological disorder that affects brain function, autism results in deficient communication skills. Autistic children live in a world of their own. Georgie's mother finally found a doctor with a special machine that manipulates sound frequencies to strengthen Georgie's hearing. Previously, loud sounds—the ocean, the motor of a car, thunder—caused her great pain, and led to her autistic behavior. Georgie had just finished a series of these auditory treatments. One evening at 6:00 P.M., Georgie suddenly asked her mother if she could go outside. Her mother hesitated; it was dark and raining heavily. But, Georgie explained, "The storm doesn't sound like a machine gun anymore." Joyfully, Georgie's mother sent her outside.

Situation
This is Georgie's first time in the rain without being bombarded with painful sounds. She rejoices and dances in the downpour.

Comments
Autism is a condition in which, among other symptoms, individuals are unable to develop relationships with others and are withdrawn into their own worlds. This moment in the rainstorm has a great deal of meaning for Georgie. It is her first time feeling like a "normal" person. For her, it is like being born; she is out of her shell and into a new life. The actor should imagine what Georgie's life had been like for the previous eleven years in order to grasp the significance of this moment. The actor might choose to play the scene *before* she goes outside. This is a true story; Georgie's mother is the author of the book.

Source: *The True Story of the Three Little Pigs,* a story by Jon Scieszk

Characters
One male or female: A wolf

Place
A courtroom

Background
For years we have heard the story of the three little pigs. But, we have yet to hear the wolf's version.

Situation
The wolf tells his side of the story to the judge. He believes that he should be exonerated.

Comments
It is preferable if the actor does not follow Scieszka's story. The actor should devise his own version of what happened. Remember: the wolf is defending his life.

Source: *Tuck Everlasting,* a novel by Natalie Babbitt

Characters
One female: Winnie Foster, ten years old

Place
Winnie's fenced-in front yard in the village of Treegap; noontime on a day in August

Background
Winnie Foster is an only child, constantly under the watchful eyes of her mother and grandmother. They never leave her alone, much less allow her to go any farther than the front yard. Winnie has been thinking about running away.

Situation
Winnie is in her front yard telling her problems to a large toad, who is squatting a few yards from her. (While she is talking to him, her grandmother is yelling at her from the house that she'll get dirty sitting on the grass.) Winnie tells the toad that she's not sure what she wants to do, but she wants to do *something*—something that would make a difference in the world. Caged up this way, she won't ever be able to do anything important. She wants to be out on her own, like the toad, free to make her own choices and decisions.

Comments
To the actor playing Winnie: say anything you want to the toad. Tell him your secrets, your dreams, your fantasies; try to get answers; get your problems off your chest. He's a pretty good listener.

See index for other improvisations from this source.

Source: *Uncle Tom's Cabin*, a novel by Harriet Beecher Stowe

Characters
One female: Eva Saint Clare, an eleven-year-old white girl

Place
The Saint Clare household in the Deep South; 1859

Background
Eva's mother suffers from headaches, and Eva's father has fallen in love with another woman. Until now, Eva was not aware of anything remotely romantic between her father and this other woman.

Situation
Eva accidentally walks into a room and finds her father passionately kissing the other woman. Aghast, Eva flees from the scene to her bedroom.

Comments
This is such a traumatic experience for Eva that she becomes very ill and eventually dies, without telling anyone of her grief. On her death bed, she makes her father promise that he will free all of the slaves. He does carry out her dying wish. The scene, in which Eva makes this last request, could be another improvisation.

Source: *Western Wind,* a novel by Paula Fox

Characters
One female: Elizabeth Benedict, eleven years old

Place
The window seat of a small airplane flying from Boston, Massachusetts, to Bangor, Maine

Background
When Elizabeth's parents were in their forties they had another child named Stephen Lindsay. They were so thrilled with Stephen Lindsay that they wanted to spend all of their time with him. Eventually, they decided to send Elizabeth to live with her grandmother in Maine.

Situation
Elizabeth is watching her parents through the small window of the airplane as it begins to taxi down the runway. At first, they appear to be arguing—perhaps about whether or not they should have sent her away—but then Stephen Lindsay diverts their attention.

Comments
Elizabeth's parents may have been justified in sending her to live with her grandmother when the new baby arrived, but their reasoning is hard for Elizabeth to understand. She feels unwanted, abandoned, and resentful of Stephen Lindsay. She believes that he took her parents away from her. She is about to start a new life with a grandmother whom she doesn't know well. This is an anxious and lonely time for Elizabeth.

See also the following improvisation.

Source: *Western Wind,* a novel by Paula Fox

Characters
One female: Elizabeth Benedict

Place
Elizabeth's grandmother's house

Background
Elizabeth's parents had a baby late in life and sent Elizabeth to live with her grandmother. Elizabeth resented being sent away, but in time she grew to love Gran. Gran was always sketching, but Elizabeth never knew precisely what.

Situation
Gran has just died, and Elizabeth returns to the house after the funeral. A friend hands her an envelope. Elizabeth opens it and finds it full of Gran's drawings. And they are all of Elizabeth—washing dishes, reading, barefoot, asleep in a chair.

Comments
These drawings bring back many memories. The actor playing Elizabeth can create the pictures through her imagination. Until this moment, Elizabeth hasn't realized how important she was to Gran.

See also the preceding improvisation.

$$\longrightarrow \blacklozenge \longleftarrow$$

6

Unusual Circumstances

The situations in this chapter may or may not be likely to occur in everyday life. Unlike fantasy, all of the situations are within the realm of possibility. Unusual circumstances may take actors to different places or periods in history with different social mores and styles. Actors will be required to deal with circumstances that may be real but new to them.

Many of the circumstances in this chapter will stretch the actors' imagination by challenging their ability to deal with the unexpected and the unfamiliar. The actors must act and react as honestly and naturally—in extraordinary circumstances—as they would in ordinary circumstances. It is the truth underneath the actors' actions and words that makes a scene work and acting believable. Regardless of how bizarre the situation or unusual the circumstance may seem, it is the actors' total devotion to the reality of a scene that allows the audience to suspend its disbelief. These situations will help actors gain the ability to create events and situations that can or might happen.

UNUSUAL CIRCUMSTANCES SITUATIONS

One male, one female
The Boy Who Talked to Whales
The Prince and the Pauper
The Trumpet of the Swan
The Wind in the Willows
The Woman Warrior

135

Two males
Secret Santa
The Whipping Boy

Ensemble
"A Debt Repaid"
He Who Says Yes and He Who Says No
The Ice Wolf: A Tale of the Eskimos
The Panda and the Spy
The Paper Bag Princess
Rats on the Roof
The Unwicked Witch

Source: *The Boy Who Talked to Whales*, a play by Webster Smalley

Characters
One male, one female: Jerry, a ten-year-old boy; Meg, an eleven-year-old girl

Place
Near the water on Puget Sound in the state of Washington

Background
Meg and Jerry are in the same class at school. They are good friends. Jerry is different from other children his age. He is a science whiz with a particular passion for whales. Meg often comes to Jerry's defense when their classmates give him a hard time. He recently got in trouble at school for criticizing research another boy had conducted on whales.

Situation
Jerry has figured out how to communicate with a whale, but he has not told anyone his secret. When Meg tries to find out why he started the fight at school, he has to decide if he will reveal his amazing discovery and show her how he talks with Ooka, the whale.

Comments
Jerry is nervous about telling his secret and also dying to share it. Meg is dying to know Jerry's secret and is more than a little amazed when it is revealed.

Source: "A Debt Repaid," a story in *Japanese Folktale Stories About Judge Ooka*, collected by Venceslava Hrdlicková and Zdenek Hrdlicka

Characters
Ensemble; Three males: Chohei, a student; Shingobei, his landlord; Judge Ooka, a wise old man

Place
A courtroom in Japan; a long time ago

Background
Chohei rents a room from Shingobei. Shingobei cooks great tempura, and Chohei can smell the fish frying in sesame oil. While he eats his dry rice, he inhales the wonderful smell of tempura. He invites a friend to join him, but Shingobei overhears this.

Situation
Shingobei becomes angry and takes Chohci to court for stealing the smell of tempura. Judge Ooka must decide how to resolve this case.

Comments
In the story, Judge Ooka has Chohei rattle some coins and asks Shingobei if he hears them. He does, so Ooka rules he has stolen the sound of Chohei's coins and calls them even.

The actor playing the judge can resolve this as he likes or he may use the solution from the actual folktale. However, he must deal with this case as seriously as if it were grand theft.

See also improvisation from the following source: "Ooka and Two Honest Men."

Source: *He Who Says Yes* and *He Who Says No*, two short German plays by Bertolt Brecht, based on a Japanese Noh play, in *All the World's a Stage: Modern Plays for Young People*, edited by Lowell Swortzell

Characters
Two males, ensemble: A young boy; his teacher; classmates

Place
The top of a mountain in Japan; many years ago

Background
An epidemic raged across Japan. The people of a certain isolated village had no medicine with which to treat those who had become ill. The school teacher and his pupils set out on a long and treacherous journey over great mountains in quest of medicine. Along the way, one boy fell ill. There is an age-old village custom that allows travelers to abandon anyone who slows their progress; the group stops to discuss the situation.

Situation
The decision must be made: either turn back, abide by tradition and abandon the boy; or kill the boy so he won't be left to die alone. The boy himself must make the decision.

Comments
Brecht wrote two versions of this story. In this version, *He Who Says Yes*, because the boy's mother and many others will die if they don't get the medicine soon, it is necessary to make the difficult choice between abandonment and merciful murder. The actor playing the boy must not be too noble or there will be little or no improvisation. No matter what the custom may be, nobody wants to die. The boy must also consider how his decision will affect his mother. In the second version, *He Who Says No*, the boy refuses to be hurled over the cliff. He insists the party turn back thereby abandoning the ancient custom. They decide to establish a new custom and the boy lives.

Source: *The Ice Wolf: A Tale of the Eskimos*, a play by Joanna Halpert Kraus

Characters
One male, one female, ensemble: Anatou, a young girl; Tarto, a young boy, Anatou's friend; Anatou's parents; villagers

Place
A small, isolated Eskimo village near Hudson Bay in Canada, before the arrival of missionaries and white men

Background
Anatou was born to Eskimo parents, but her skin was pale and her hair was blonde. This was a phenomenon in the village; everyone else was dark-haired and dark-skinned. The people believed that Anatou was an evil spirit and the cause of all the misfortune that befell the village.

Situation
Here are several interesting situations from the play, offered in chronological order.

> One male, one female, ensemble: Anatou's father, Anatou's
> mother; townspeople
> When Anatou was a baby, the townspeople attempted to persuade
> her parents to kill her because of the evil spells they believed she
> would cast on the village. Anatou's parents don't want to kill their
> child—but neither do they want to leave the village, their only home.

> One female, ensemble: Anatou, a young girl; townspeople
> Anatou made a beautiful pair of boots for her father. He was wearing
> these boots when he set out with Anatou's mother to search for food
> in a blizzard. Her parents have been gone for a long time and are be-
> lieved to be lost. Everyone accuses Anatou of having put a curse on
> her father's boots, claiming that she is responsible for killing her own
> parents by witchcraft. They want her to leave the village. But Anatou
> is all alone now, without any parents. What can she do?

> One male, one female: Anatou, a young girl; Tarto, a young boy
> Tarto, Anatou's only friend, begins to believe that she is causing
> all the problems in the village. The hunters keep returning with
> empty sleds; the villagers are starving. Anatou tries to convince
> Tarto that she is not responsible for every bad thing that happens
> in the village.

Comments
This play is about fear, hate, and love. The actors should try to accept the
beliefs of the Eskimos of that time. There are people *today* who fear others who look different from themselves and believe that they are evil. This
is still one cause of war and urban violence today.

Source: *The Panda and the Spy*, a play
by Mary Virginia Heinlein

Characters
Two females, one male: Mandy Allen, age six; Goofy, her elder sister;
Rickey, her elder brother

Place
The living room of a suburban home

Background
Lately, the Allen's living room has been getting turned upside-down. Mandy knows that the culprit is the panda bear who escaped from the circus and took up residence in the root cellar under the trap door in the Allen's living room. Although she tells her parents the truth, she is reluctant to show them the panda for fear that it will be sent back to the circus. Everyone in the family thinks that Mandy has an overactive imagination.

Situation
Rickey and Goofy find Mandy rushing around the living room, trying to straighten up after another "attack" by the panda, for which her family believes she is responsible. Rickey and Goofy, nonbelievers regarding the panda, confront Mandy about her behavior. Mandy swears her brother and sister to secrecy and reveals the panda who is sleeping in the root cellar under the trap door in the floor.

Comments
Mandy shares her secret in order to enlist Rickey and Goofy's support in hiding the panda. While she takes the bear's presence for granted, her brother and sister are amazed. They need to establish their own relationship to the panda and figure out how they will act to keep the secret. Another actor could be used to play the panda.

Source: *The Paper Bag Princess,* a book by Robert Munsch

Characters
Ensemble; One female, one male, one male or female: Princess Elizabeth; Prince Ronald; a dragon

Place
A kingdom; long ago and far away

Background
Elizabeth, a feisty and clever princess, was engaged to be married to the obnoxious and shallow Prince Ronald. One dark day, a dragon appeared in the kingdom, burned down the castle and all its contents with one hot breath, and flew off with Ronald. The resourceful Elizabeth made a dress for herself out of a paper bag and went in search of the dragon and her fiancé.

Situation
Elizabeth has located the dragon's cave. She knocks on the door. The dragon emerges. Relying only on her wits, Elizabeth must convince the

dragon to release Ronald and to let them both leave unharmed. She is alone, weaponless, and wearing a paper bag.

Comments

The actor playing Elizabeth must realize that she is a 1990s kind of princess. She is an independent problem-solver. Her personality characteristics must be true to life despite the fantastic nature of the story. The actor playing the dragon should find out why he refuses to release the prince. What would it take to persuade the dragon to release Ronald?

Source: *The Prince and the Pauper*, a dramatization by Aurand Harris of the novel by Samuel L. Clemens (Mark Twain)

Characters

One male, one female: Tom Conty, a ten-year-old pauper; Lady Jane, a "royal," about the same age

Place

London, England; 1547

Background

Two baby boys were born at the same time: one was Prince of Wales, heir to the throne of England; the other was Tom Conty, son of a pauper. The two boys looked as much alike as twins. Ten years later they met quite by accident. They exchanged clothes and, as a result, the true prince, believed to be the pauper, was thrown out of the palace, while the pauper, believed to be the prince, was left inside.

Situation

Tom, dressed as the prince, waits for the real prince to return. Instead, Lady Jane, the prince's best friend and only playmate, arrives to play. Afraid that he will be punished for masquerading as the prince, Tom tries to hide. Lady Jane only thinks he is playing a new game. Slowly, he reveals his true identity.

Comments

The actor playing Lady Jane has every reason to believe that Tom is the prince. Therefore, she is most concerned with his odd behavior. Tom wants his true identity known, but he fears the consequences. As the situation unfolds, Tom should come to realize the implications of his false identity.

Source: *Rats on the Roof,* short fiction by James Marshall

Characters
Ensemble; One male or one female, ensemble: A homeowner; any number of cats—Persian cats, Siamese cats, Angora cats, alley cats, kittens

Place
A house full of rats

Background
The owner of a rat-infested house advertised in the newspaper for a cat.

Situation
The owner holds interviews with a variety of cats, trying to find the best feline for the job.

Comments
Each actor takes on a different personality for each cat. The personalities should be distinctive. The owner can decide which cat he wants to hire. The problem is very serious to him, and the interviews should be businesslike.

Source: *Secret Santa,* a film by Matthew D. Huffman, Tisch School of the Arts, New York University

Characters
Two males: A middle-aged man dressed as Santa Claus; Ben, a boy about seven years old

Place
The living room of Ben's house; a few days before Christmas, early evening

Background
A bank robber dressed in a Santa Claus suit was fleeing from the crime scene when his car overheated. He escaped into the woods, but promptly collided with a tree and fell to the ground, unconscious. Danny, a little boy who had missed the school bus and was walking home through the woods, came upon the unconscious Santa. When the robber revived, Danny brought him to his house. "Santa" hid out there for a few days, having explained to Danny that he was in a little trouble with Mrs. Claus.
     Of course Danny believed that the bank robber was Santa Claus. He told Santa about Ben, a schoolmate, who beat him up every day and took his lunch money while the other kids laughed. Danny asked Santa for

help. So, one evening when Danny's parents and Ben's parents went out together (leaving the boys with baby sitters who spent the evening on the telephone), Santa paid a little visit to Ben.

Situation
Ben, the bully, sees Santa Claus in his living room and asks him what he is doing there so early. Santa says that he did not receive Ben's Christmas list this year; Ben runs to his room and retrieves it. Santa asks if he's been a good boy, and Ben replies with an emphatic, "Yes." Santa questions him about his mean treatment of Danny, and Ben admits to it at last. Santa tells him that if it happens again, Ben will not get any presents.

Comments
The actor playing Santa should bear in mind that he is really a bank robber; he is not used to talking to little boys in the manner one might expect of Santa Claus. He has grown fond of Danny and wants to repay the boy's kindness by helping Danny resolve his problem with Ben. For Ben, meeting Santa Claus in person is an important event.

Source: *The Trumpet of the Swan,* a novel by E.B. White

Characters
One male, one female: Louis, a young, male trumpeter swan; Serena, a young, female trumpeter swan

Place
Red Rocks Lake National Wildlife Refuge, Montana

Background
Louis has a handicap. He cannot make a sound; he can't even trumpet. He has learned to communicate by writing on a slate, which he wears around his neck.

Situation
One day, Serena, a beautiful swan, appears, emitting the soft sounds swans usually make. Louis, totally smitten, approaches her and bows. She greets him in a most receptive manner, but he can only communicate with her by writing on his slate. Alas, Serena cannot read.

Comments
In the book, Serena is not at all interested in a swan that cannot trumpet and spurns Louis, who is crushed by the rejection. Each actor will need

to show the frustration at not being able to be understood. Each actor needs to resolve, in any way that seems right, the inability to communicate with each other.

Source: *The Unwicked Witch,* a play by Madge Miller

Characters
Ensemble; Two males, three females: Luke; Sad Simon, his grandfather; Gobble, the old witch; Hobble, the older witch; Wobble, the oldest witch

Place
An uninhabited house

Background
Luke and his grandfather have been searching for the tune Sad Simon lost many years earlier that allows him to play his fiddle. One day, they came upon a house in great disrepair that appeared to be uninhabited. In fact, it was home to Gobble, Hobble, and Wobble, the unwashed witches. Simon and Luke decided to stay a couple of days in the house.

Situation
When the three witches discover that Luke and Simon are spending the night in the house, they decide to make their lives miserable. They assemble a collection of bottles and boxes, the contents of which will make the mortals wheeze, sneeze, twitch, itch, dance, and prance. Luke and Simon awake to start their day. Of course, the witches cannot be seen by Luke and Simon.

Comments
The actors playing Luke and Simon, totally innocent, carry on in as normal a fashion as possible, but incorporate the many tricks played on them by the witches as if they didn't know their source. It will take special concentration to react spontaneously to the witches' deeds. The witches are as dedicated to their goal as they are amused by the effect of what they do.

Source: *The Whipping Boy,* a novel by Sid Fleischman

Characters
Two males: Prince Brat; Jemmy, the royal whipping boy

Place
A palace; long ago

Background

Jemmy was an orphan who was found on the streets and taken into the castle to be the prince's whipping boy. Since it is forbidden to spank the heir to the throne, Jemmy gets the beating whenever the prince misbehaves. And the prince misbehaves a lot! Prince Brat has never been spanked in his life, so he suffers no consequences when he does something wrong.

Examples of the things the prince has done that resulted in the whipping boy's punishment include: The prince tied the wigs of the king's guests to the backs of their chairs so that when they stood up to toast the king their wigs came flying off, leaving them bare-headed. The prince burst out laughing, which made the king so angry that he called for the whipping boy. Also, the prince never did his lessons; he told his tutor he could always get someone else to read and to write for him—Jemmy. His tutor would become so angry that he would call for the whipping boy. This continued day after day.

Situation

Jemmy has just gotten twenty whacks for one of the prince's pranks, and he never uttered a sound during the beating. This infuriates the prince; he tells Jemmy that he is supposed to bawl when he gets hit. But Jemmy is determined never to give the prince that satisfaction. He hates being the whipping boy and begs the prince to stop acting up. The prince threatens to throw Jemmy out if he doesn't cry. However, when he realizes that this is just what Jemmy wants—to be thrown out—the prince warns him that if he attempts to escape he'll be tracked down and severely punished.

Comments

Jemmy is under the king's rule. He cannot be insubordinate, although he freely expresses his opinions to the prince. Jemmy has learned to read and write (he does the prince's lessons for him), but Prince Brat is illiterate. The actor playing Jemmy has a sense of his own identity, but he must accept that he is a prisoner in the palace. Although he may try to escape, they'll always find him. The actor playing the prince can simply enjoy being a brat.

See also the following improvisation.

Source: *The Whipping Boy,* a novel by Sid Fleischman

Characters
Two males: Prince Brat; Jemmy, the royal whipping boy

Place
A palace; long ago

Background
Jemmy, an orphan, was found on the streets and brought into the castle to be the royal whipping boy. Whenever the prince misbehaves, Jemmy takes a beating; it is forbidden to spank the heir to the throne. Prince Brat has never been spanked in his life, so he has nothing to fear when he does something bad. And he constantly misbehaves.

Situation
One night the prince tells Jemmy that he is bored and wants Jemmy to run away with him. Jemmy doesn't want to run away; he knows that the king will hunt them down and punish the whipping boy severely, and Prince Brat will be unharmed. Jemmy attempts to talk the prince out of his plan.

Comments
In many ways, Jemmy is superior to the prince (he can read and write, but the prince is illiterate; he clearly has a better sense of responsibility and ethics than does the prince). However, the prince wields the power in this relationship, and both boys know it. In the novel, the prince insists that he and Jemmy run away. Jemmy, far more ingenious than the prince, gets them out of many scrapes. Two highwaymen, who mistake the prince for the whipping boy, capture them. When the prince receives a whipping, his attitude toward Jemmy changes, and they become friends.

        See also the preceding improvisation.

Source: *The Wind in the Willows,* a novel by Kenneth Grahame

Characters
One male, one female: Toad, an English country gentleman; Penelope, a young woman

Place
The dungeon of a castle in the English countryside

Background
Always chasing the latest fad, Toad fell in love with motor cars and motoring. He bought and wrecked one car after another (behind the steering wheel he became a toad possessed), until his friends finally prevailed upon him to promise never to buy another car. However, Toad was unable to resist the lure of the open road. He was arrested and sentenced to twenty years in jail for stealing a limousine, speeding, and insulting a po-

liceman. While in prison, he made friends with the jailer's daughter, Penelope, who finds Toad dashing and debonair.

Situation
Penelope believes that jail is no place for Toad. She devises a clever plan for the prisoner's escape. She brings her aunt's clothes to Toad and dresses him as her aunt, a washer woman who comes and goes from the jail every day with laundry basket in hand. While Toad sneaks away dressed in the washer woman's bonnet and skirt, Penelope waits in Toad's cell, bound and gagged as if Toad had overwhelmed her.

Comments
Because the disguise is at the heart of the improvisation, the actors should come prepared with appropriate washer woman garb to make the most of the dressing up process.

   The actors playing Toad and Penelope are completely serious with one another especially in their efforts to pull the wool over the eyes of the law. The actor playing Toad must keep in mind that he is at least a bit of an upper-class snob, a self-indulgent and entitled creature despite his winning ways. Neither Toad nor Penelope should seem to be aware that their situation is monumentally absurd.

Source: *The Woman Warrior: Memoirs of a Girlhood Among Ghosts,* by Maxine Hong Kingston (improvisation written by UCLA theatre student Ryan Cadiz)

Characters
One female, one male: A ten-year-old Chinese-American girl; a white pharmacist

Place
A drugstore in Stockton, California

Background
The girl struggles, vacillating between, feeling more American than Chinese and at other times feeling more Chinese than American. Her mother compounds her confusion by telling strange, supernatural stories of days back in China. This alternately pushes her away from her heritage by puzzling her and draws her closer by making her realize that she identifies with her mother's stories.

   A delivery man arrived at her family's home to drop off a large package—a box of prescription medicine. However, the family had not ordered any medicine. The mother, extremely superstitious, believed that the mistaken delivery of medicine was a ploy of the "white ghost," the pharmacist, to bring harmful spirits of sickness into their household. She commanded her daughter to return the box to the drugstore and to demand candy as reparation for the pharmacist's attempt to put illness and bad spirits upon the family.

Situation

The daughter reluctantly returns the box to the pharmacist. Her mother has warned her that she will not be let back into the house unless she brings back free candy as an apology from the pharmacist, so that the family can ward off sickness. The daughter tries to explain her situation to the pharmacist, even though she does not fully understand it. The girl is not sure whether she should disregard her mother's old-world ways or whether to believe that her family's health actually relies on her getting something sweet to expel disease. The white druggist is confused by the girl's frantic pleas, but is also amused by the superstitions of the "foreign" Chinese who have flooded into Stockton; he may even think that the young girl is speaking in another tongue.

Comments

Whether or not the girl believes that her mother's old-world convictions do not apply in America, the land of her birth, she cannot return to her home empty-handed. Her mother is a powerful, although loving, woman who cannot be disappointed or disobeyed. Also, assume that the daughter has no money with which she could buy the candy herself.

BIBLIOGRAPHY

Professional Resources

Chekhov, M. 1985. *Lessons for the Professional Actor*. New York: Performing Arts Journal Publications.

Hagen, U. 1991. *A Challenge for the Actor*. New York: Scribner.

Nachmanovitch, S. 1990. *Free Play: Improvisation in Life and Art*. Los Angeles: Tarcher.

Shurtleff, M. 1978. *Audition: Everything an Actor Needs to Know to Get the Part*. New York: Walker.

Stanislavski, C. 1936. *An Actor Prepares*. Trans. E. R. Hapgood. New York: Theatre Arts Books.

_____.1949. *Building a Character*. Trans. E. R. Hapgood. New York: Theatre Arts Books.

Strasberg, L. 1965. *Strasberg at the Actors Studio*. R. H. Hethmon, ed. New York: Viking.

Thomas, J. 1993. "Empowering the Actor with Stanislavski's Method of Active Analysis." Paper presented at the SETC conference, Arlington, Virginia, March, 1993.

Zeder, S. 1988. *In a Room Somewhere*. New Orleans: Anchorage Press.

Literary Works

Alcott, L. M. 1965. *Little Women*. Racine, WI: Whitman.

Allen, J. P. 1969. *The Prime of Miss Jean Brodie, a Drama in Three Acts*. New York: Samuel French.

Andersen, H. C. 1949. *The Emperor's New Clothes*. New York: Houghton Mifflin.

Angelou, M. "The Reunion." In *Hot and Cool: Jazz Short Stories*. M. Breton, ed. New York: New American Library.

Anouilh, J. 1956. *The Lark*. Adapted by L. Hellman. New York: Random House.

Atiyeh, W. 1955. *Ali Baba and the Forty Thieves*. Anchorage, KY: Children's Theatre Press.

Atwater, F., and R. Atwater. 1938. *Mr. Popper's Penguins*. Boston: Little, Brown.

Austen, J. 1993. *Emma*. New York: Norton.

Avery, H. 1981. *The Secret Garden*. New Orleans: Anchorage Press.

Babbitt, N. 1975. *Tuck Everlasting*. New York: Farrar, Straus & Giroux.

Barrie, J. M. 1980. *Peter Pan*. New York: Scribner.

Baum, L. F. 1979. *The Wizard of Oz*. New York: Ballantine.

"Beautiful Brown Eyes." 1993. In *African-American Folktales for Young Readers*. Collected by R. Young and J. Dockrey Young. Little Rock: August House.

Blume, J. 1972. *Tales of a Fourth Grade Nothing*. New York: Dutton.

————. 1985. *Freckle Juice*. New York: Macmillan.

Boublil, A. and G. M. Shonberg. *Miss Saigon*

Bradley, A., and M. Bond. 1974. *The Adventures of a Bear Called Paddington*. London: Samuel French.

Brecht B. 1972. "He Who Says Yes." In *All the World's a Stage: Modern Plays for Young People*. L. Swortzell, ed. New York: Delacorte.

————. 1972. "He Who Says No." In *All the World's a Stage: Modern Plays for Young People*. L. Swortzell, ed. New York: Delacorte.

Brontë, C. 1987. *Jane Eyre*. New York: Bantam.

Brooks, M. 1993. "A Boy and His Dog." In *Who Do You Think You Are?: Stories of Friends and Enemies*. Selected by H. Rochman and D. Z. McCampbell. Boston: Little, Brown.

Burnett, F. H. 1962. *The Secret Garden*. New York: Dell.

————. 1985. *A Little Princess*. New York: Lippincott.

Butler, O. 1988. *Kindred*. Boston: Beacon Press.

Carcaterra, L. 1995. *Sleepers*. New York: Ballantine.

Carroll, L. 1977. *Alice's Adventures in Wonderland*. New York: St. Martin's Press.

Chekhov, A. 1986. *The Seagull: A Comedy in Four Acts*. Trans. M. Frayn. London: Methuen.

Chikamatsu, M. 1979. *Heike Nyogo No Shima*. In *The Art of Kabuki, Famous Plays in Performance*. Translated and with commentary by S. L. Leiter. Berkley: University of California Press.

Childress, A. 1986. *Wedding Band.* In *Nine Plays by Black Women.* M. B. Wilkerson, ed. New York: New American Library.

Chocolate, D. 1996. *A Very Special Kwanzaa.* New York: Scholastic.

Chopin, K. 1984. "Desiree's Baby" and "The Story of an Hour." In *The Awakening and Selected Stories.* S. M. Gilbert, ed. New York: Penguin.

Cisneros, S. 1991. "Geraldo No Last Name." In *The House on Mango Street.* New York: Vintage.

Clarke, J. H. 1993. "The Boy Who Painted Christ Black." In *Black American Short Stories: One Hundred Years of the Best.* J. H. Clarke, ed. New York: Hill and Wang.

Danziger, P. 1974. *The Cat Ate My Gymsuit.* New York: Dell.

de Brunhoff, J. 1985. *The Travels of Babar.* Trans. M. S. Haas. New York: Random House.

de Marivaux, P. 1723. *Changes in Heart* (Double Inconstancy). Translated by Steven Wadsworth. Paris: Flagault.

Dickens, C. 1987. *The Posthumous Papers of the Pickwick Club.* New York: Oxford University Press.

_____ . 1992. *Great Expectations.* New York: Knopf.

Dorfman, A. 1990. "The Rebellion of the Magical Rabbits." In *Where Angels Glide at Dawn: New Stories From Latin America.* L. M. Carlson and C. L. Ventura, eds. New York: Lippincott.

_____ . 1992. *Death and the Maiden.* New York: Penguin.

Dorris, M. 1987. *A Yellow Raft in Blue Water.* New York: Henry Holt.

Douglass, F. 1994. *Escape From Slavery: The Boyhood of Frederick Douglass in His Own Words.* M. McCurdy, ed. New York: Knopf.

Du Maurier, D. 1965. *Rebecca.* New York: Modern Library.

Engar, K. M. 1967. *Arthur and the Magic Sword.* In *Twenty Plays for Young People: A Collection of Plays for Children.* Compiled by W. M. Birner. Anchorage, KY: Anchorage Press.

Faulkner, W. 1979. "The Bear." In *Uncollected Stories of William Faulkner.* J. Blotner, ed. New York: Random House.

Feiffer, J. 1993. *The Man in the Ceiling.* New York: Michael DiCapua Books.

Ferber, E., and G. S. Kaufman. 1939. *Stage Door.* In *Twenty Best Plays of the Modern American Theatre.* J. Gassner, ed. New York: Crown.

Fielding, H. 1970. *The Tragedy of Tragedies, or The Life and Death of Tom Thumb the Great, with the Annotations of H. Scriblerus Secundus.* J. T. Hillhouse, ed. St. Clair Shores, MI: Scholarly Press.

Fisher, S. 1980. *The Tale of the Shining Princess.* From a translation of the story by D. Keene. New York: Metropolitan Museum of Art/Viking Press.

Fleischman, S. 1986. *The Whipping Boy*. New York: Greenwillow.

Fox, P. 1993. *Western Wind*. New York: Orchard.

Fritz, J. 1958. *The Cabin Faced West*. New York: Coward-McCann.

Fry, R. K. 1995. *The Secret of Roan Inish*. New York: Hyperion.

Fugard, A. 1996. *Valley Song*. New York: Theatre Communications Group.

Galati, F. 1991. *John Steinbeck's The Grapes of Wrath*. New York: Dramatists Play Service.

Gallico, P. 1958. *Mrs. 'Arris Goes to Paris*. Garden City, NY: Doubleday.

García Márquez, G. 1983. *Chronicle of a Death Foretold*. Trans. G. Rabassa. New York: Knopf.

Geiogamah, H. 1994. *Coon Cons Coyote*. In *Hanay Geiogamah: Teatro*. Trans. Annamaria Pinazzi. Rome: Castlevecchi.

Gibson, W. 1960. *The Miracle Worker: A Play in Three Acts*. New York: Samuel French.

Gonzalez, R. 1994. "The Boiler Room." In *Nuestro New York: An Anthology of Puerto Rican Plays*. J. V. Antush, ed. New York: Penguin.

Goodrich, F., and A. Hackett. 1956. *The Diary of Anne Frank*. A dramatization based on *Anne Frank: Diary of a Young Girl*. New York: Random House.

Grahame, K. 1983. *The Wind in the Willows*. New York: Scribner.

Gray, N. S. 1951. *The Tinder-Box, a Play for Children*. London: Dennis Dobson.

Gurney, A. R. 1996. *Sylvia*. New York: Dramatists Play Service.

Hall, R. 1973. "The Princess of the Sea." In *Three Tales from Japan: Three Dramatized Folk Tales for Children*. Anchorage, KY: Anchorage Press.

Hamilton, V. 1965. "Doc Rabbit, Bruh Fox, and Tar Baby" and "The Lion, Bruh Bear, and Bruh Rabbit." In *The People Could Fly: American Black Folktales Told by Virginia Hamilton*. New York: Knopf.

———. 1995. "The Mer-Woman Out of the Sea." In *Her Stories: African-American Folktales, Fairy Tales, and True Tales*. New York: Blue Sky Press.

Harling, R. 1988. *Steel Magnolias*. New York: Dramatists Play Service.

Harris, A. 1980. *The Arkansaw Bear*. New Orleans: Anchorage Press.

———. 1989. *The Pinballs*. New Orleans: Anchorage Press.

———. 1991. *A Doctor in Spite of Himself*. In *Short Plays of Theatre Classics*. A. Harris, ed. New Orleans: Anchorage Press.

Heinlein, M. V. 1954. *The Panda and the Spy*. Anchorage, KY: Children's Theatre Press.

Hellman, L. 1972. *The Children's Hour*. In *Collected Plays*. S. M. Gilbert, ed. Boston: Little, Brown.

Henkes, K. 1995. *Protecting Marie*. New York: Greenwillow.

Hijuelos, O. 1992. *The Mambo Kings Sing Songs of Love*. New York: Harper Perennial.

Homer. 1996. *The Odyssey*. Trans. R. Fagles. New York: Viking.

Houston, V. H. 1993. *The Matsuyama Mirror*. In *Short Plays for Young Actors*. C. Slaight and J. Sharrar, eds. Lyme, NH: Smith and Kraus.

Hrdlicková, V., and Z. Hrdlicka. 1993. *Japanese Folktale Stories About Judge Ooka*. Prague: Aventinum.

Hugo, V. 1887. *Les Misérables*. Trans. I. F. Hapgood. New York: Thomas Y. Crowell.

———. 1937. *Notre-Dame de Paris,* or *The Hunchback of Notre Dame*. New York: Book League of America.

Hwang, D. H. 1996. *M Butterfly*. In *The Harcourt Brace Anthology of Drama*. 2d ed. Compiled by W. B. Worthen. Fort Worth, TX: Harcourt Brace College.

Ishiguro, K. 1990. *The Remains of the Day*. New York: Vintage.

Jones, L. 1964. *Dutchman, and The Slave*. New York: Morrow Quill.

Kaestner, E. 1934. *Emil and the Detectives: A Children's Play in Three Acts*. Adapt. C. Brooke. London: Samuel French.

Kalidasa. 1967. *Shakuntala*. In *A Treasury of the Theatre*. J. Gassner, ed. New York: Simon and Schuster.

Keneally, T. 1982. *Schindler's List*. New York: Simon and Schuster.

Kincaid, J. 1996. *The Autobiography of My Mother*. New York: Farrar, Straus & Giroux.

Kingston, M. H. 1989. *The Woman Warrior: Memoirs of a Girlhood Among Ghosts*. New York: Vintage.

Kraus, J. H. 1963. *The Ice Wolf: A Tale of the Eskimos, A Play for Young People in Three Acts*. Rowayton, CT: New Plays for Children.

Lee, H. 1960. *To Kill a Mockingbird*. Philadelphia: Lippincott.

L'Engle, M. 1960. *Meet the Austins*. New York: Vanguard.

———. 1964. *The Moon by Night*. New York: Ariel Books.

———. 1965. *Camilla*. New York: Thomas Y. Crowell.

Lessing, D. 1988. "The Old Chief Mshlanga." In *Somehow Tenderness Survives: Stories of Southern Africa*. Compiled by H. Rochman. New York: Harper and Row.

———. 1988. "A Sunrise on the Veld." In *The Doris Lessing Reader*. New York: Alfred A. Knopf.

Lewis, C. S. 1970. *The Lion, the Witch, and the Wardrobe.* The *Chronicles of Narnia* Series. New York: Collier.

Lewis, E. F. 1953. *To Beat a Tiger, One Needs a Brother's Help.* New York: Holt, Rhinehart and Winston.

Lindgren, A. 1950. *Pippi Longstocking.* Trans. F. Lamborn. New York: Viking.

Lionni, L. 1967. *Frederick.* New York: Pantheon.

———. 1970. *Fish Is Fish.* New York: Pantheon.

———. 1993. *Swimmy.* New York: Scholastic.

Lowry, L. 1993. *The Giver.* Boston: Houghton Mifflin.

MacDonald, B. B. 1975. *Mrs. Piggle-Wiggle.* New York: Lippincott.

MacLachlan, P. 1985. *Sarah, Plain and Tall.* New York: Harper and Row.

———. 1991. *Journey.* New York: Delacorte.

———. 1993. *Baby.* New York: Delacorte.

Maeterlinck, M. 1912a. *Péllèas and Mélisande.* New York: Dodd, Mead.

———. 1912b. *The Blue Bird.* New York: Dodd, Mead.

Marshall, J. 1991. *Rats on the Roof.* New York: Dial.

Martin, R. 1992. *The Rough-Face Girl.* New York: Putnam.

Mason, B. A. 1985. *In Country.* New York: Harper and Row.

McCully, E. A. 1992. *Mirette on the High Wire.* New York: Putnam.

Miller, M. 1964. *The Unwicked Witch.* Anchorage, KY: Anchorage Press.

Miller, S. 1987. *Inventing the Abbotts and Other Stories.* New York: Harper and Row.

Milne, A. A. 1926. *Winnie-the-Pooh.* New York: E. P. Dutton.

Molnar, F. 1960. *Liliom.* In *A Treasury of the Theatre: From Henrik Ibsen to Eugene Ionesco.* J. Gassner, ed. New York: Simon and Schuster.

Montgomery, L. M. 1983. *Anne of Green Gables.* New York: Grosset and Dunlap.

Munsch, R. 1981. *The Paper Bag Princess.* Toronto: Annick Press.

Myers, W. D. 1988. *Scorpions.* New York: Harper and Row.

Naylor, P. R. 1991. *Shiloh.* New York: Macmillan.

Nightingale: A Participatory Play for Children. 1983. Adapted from H. C. Andersen's story by J. Urquhart, R. Grossberg, and Yellow Brick Road Shows. New Orleans: Anchorage Press.

Norris, J. 1968. *Aladdin and the Wonderful Lamp.* New Orleans: Anchorage Press.

O'Brien, T. 1984. *Going After Cacciato.* New York: Dell.

O'Connor, F. "Masculine Protest." In *Collected Stories.* New York: Alfred A. Knopf.

O'Neill, E. 1996. *Ah, Wilderness!* In *The Harcourt Brace Anthology of Drama.* Compiled by W. B. Worthen. Fort Worth, TX: Harcourt Brace College.

Ortiz-Cofer, J. 1993. "American History." In *Who Do You Think You Are? Stories of Friends and Enemies.* H. Rochman and D. Z. McCampbell, eds. Boston: Little, Brown.

Paterson, K. 1978. *The Great Gilly Hopkins.* New York: Thomas Y. Crowell.

Paulsen, G. 1993. *Nightjohn.* New York: Delacorte.

Payne, E. 1944. *Katy No-Pocket.* Boston: Houghton Mifflin.

Perry, R. 1969. *The Emperor's New Clothes.* Chicago: Dramatic Publishing.

Porter, C. 1993a. *Happy Birthday Addy!: A Springtime Story.* Middleton, WI: Pleasant Company.

———. 1993b. *Addy Learns a Lesson: A School Story.* Middleton, WI: Pleasant Company.

———. 1993c. *Addy's Surprise: A Christmas Story.* Middleton, WI: Pleasant Company.

———. 1993d. *Meet Addy: An American Girl.* Middleton, WI: Pleasant Company.

———. 1994a. *Addy Saves the Day: A Summer Story.* Middleton, WI: Pleasant Company.

———. 1994b. *Changes for Addy: A Winter Story.* Middleton, WI: Pleasant Company.

Potter, B. 1987. *The Tale of Peter Rabbit.* London: Frederick Warne.

———. 1991. *The Tale of Jemima Puddle-Duck.* London: Frederick Warne.

Prejean, H. 1993. *Dead Man Walking: An Eyewitness Account of the Death Penalty in the United States.* New York: Random House.

Raphaelson, S. 1983. *The Shop Around the Corner.* In *Three Screen Comedies.* Wisconsin Center for Film and Theater Research. Madison: University of Wisconsin Press.

Ribman, R. 1978. *The Journey of the Fifth Horse.* In *Five Plays.* New York: Avon.

Rylant, C. 1985. *A Blue-Eyed Daisy.* New York: Bradbury.

———. 1990. "A Crush." In *A Couple of Kooks, and Other Stories About Love.* New York: Orchard.

Sacks, O. W. 1983. *Awakenings.* New York: Dutton.

Salinger, J. D. 1980. *The Catcher in the Rye.* New York: Bantam.

Santos, B. 1979. "Immigration Blues," "Manilla House," and "Footnote to a Laundry List." In *Scent of Apples: A Collection of Stories.* Seattle: University of Washington Press.

Satchell, M. 1994. *Langston Hughes: Poet of the People.* In *The Big Book of*

Large-Cast Plays: Twenty-Seven One-Act Plays for Young Actors. S. E. Kamerman, ed. Boston: Plays, Inc.

Schenkkan, R. 1994. *The Kentucky Cycle*. New York: Dramatists Play Service.

Scieszka, J. 1989. *The True Story of the Three Little Pigs*. New York: Viking Kestrel.

———. 1991. *The Frog Prince Continued*. New York: Viking.

Scieszka, J., and L. Smith. 1992. *The Stinky Cheese Man and Other Fairly Stupid Tales*. New York: Viking.

Seeger, P. 1986. *Abiyoyo*. New York: Macmillan.

Shakespeare, W. 1966. *The Plays and Poems of William Shakespeare*. New York: AMS Press.

Shue, L. 1985. *The Foreigner*. New York: Dramatists Play Service.

Smalley, W. 1981. *The Boy Who Talked to Whales*. New Orleans: Anchorage Press.

Sophocles. 1990. *Antigone*. In *Classic Tragedy, Greek and Roman: Eight Plays in Authoritative Modern Translations*. R. W. Corrigan, ed. New York: Applause Theatre.

Soto, G. 1991. *A Summer Life*. New York: Dell.

Stehli, A. 1991. *The Sound of a Miracle: A Child's Triumph over Autism*. New York: Doubleday.

Steinbeck, J. 1939. *The Grapes of Wrath*. New York: Penguin.

———. 1965. *Of Mice and Men*. New York: Modern Library.

———. 1975. *The Pearl*. New York: Bantam.

Stowe, H. B. 1969. *Uncle Tom's Cabin*. Columbus, OH: Merrill.

Swift, G. 1983. *Waterland*. London: Heinemann.

Swortzell, L. 1994a. *Cinderella, The World's Favorite Fairy Tale*. Charlottesville, VA: New Plays.

———. 1994b. *The Mischief Makers*. Charlottesville, VA: New Plays.

———. 1995. *The Shepherds of Saint Francis*. Woodstock, IL: Dramatic Publishing.

Tale of the Shining Princess, The. 1980. A Japanese tale adapted by S. Fisher from a translation of the story by D. Keene. New York: Metropolitan Museum of Art/Viking Press.

Tan, A. 1989. *The Joy Luck Club*. New York: Putnam.

———. 1991. *The Kitchen God's Wife*. New York: Putnam.

Thomas, J. 1987. *Newcomer*. New Orleans: Anchorage Press.

Tolstoy, L. 1961. *Anna Karenina*. Trans. D. Magarshack. New York: New American Library.

Treadwell, S. 1949. *Machinal, Episode Three: Honeymoon*. In *Twenty-Five*

Best Plays of the Modern American Theatre: Early Series. J. Gassner, ed. New York: Crown.

Tripp, V. 1991. *Meet Felicity: An American Girl.* Middleton, WI: Pleasant Company.

Truman, M. 1995. "Christmas Eve with the Trumans." In *First Ladies.* A Fawcett Columbine Book. New York: Ballantine.

Twain, M. 1946. *Tom Sawyer.* Cleveland: World.

_____. 1964. *The Prince and the Pauper.* New York: Heritage Press.

Uchida, Y. 1971. *Journey to Topaz: A Story of the Japanese-American Evacuation.* New York: Scribner.

_____. 1978. *Journey Home.* New York: Atheneum.

Villanueva-Collado, A. 1990. "The Day We Went to See Snow." In *Where Angels Glide at Dawn: New Stories from Latin America.* L. M. Carlson and C. L. Ventura, eds. New York: J. B. Lippincott.

"Vilma Martinez." In *Notable Hispanic Women.* D. Felgen and J. Kamp, eds. Gale Research.

Vine, B. 1987. *A Dark-Adapted Eye.* New York: Bantam.

Viorst, J. 1972. *Alexander and the Terrible, Horrible, No Good, Very Bad Day.* New York: Atheneum.

Waber, B. 1972. *Ira Sleeps Over.* Boston: Houghton Mifflin.

Walker, A. 1983. *The Color Purple.* New York: Pocket Books.

Walter, M. P. 1986. *Justin and the Best Biscuits in the World.* New York: Lothrop, Lee and Shepard.

Ward, L. 1952. *The Biggest Bear.* Boston: Houghton Mifflin.

West, D. 1995. *The Wedding.* New York: Doubleday.

Wharton, W. 1979. *Birdy.* New York: Knopf.

White, E. B. 1945. *Stuart Little.* New York: Harper and Brothers.

_____. 1952. *Charlotte's Web.* New York: Harper and Row.

_____. 1970. *The Trumpet of the Swan.* New York: Harper and Row.

Wilder, T. 1941. *Our Town.* In *Sixteen Famous American Plays.* B. A. Cerf and V. H. Cartmell, eds. New York: Modern Library.

_____. 1972. *Childhood.* In *All the World's a Stage: Modern Plays for Young People.* L. Swortzell, ed. New York: Delacorte.

Williams, M. B. 1985. *The Velveteen Rabbit.* New York: Knopf.

Woolf, V. 1992. "The New Dress." In *That Kind of Woman.* B. Adams and T. Tate, eds. New York: Carroll and Graf.

Zeder, S. L. 1990. *Doors* and *In a Room Somewhere.* In *Wish in One Hand, Spit in the Other: A Collection of Plays.* S. Pearson-Dans, ed. New Orleans: Anchorage Press.

Zubizarreta, R., H. Rohmer, and D. Schecter. 1991. *The Woman Who Outshone the Sun: The Legend of Lucia Zenteno*. From a poem by A. C. Martinez. New York: Scholastic.

Films, Unpublished Plays, and Screenplays

Ah, Wilderness! 1935. MGM. Clarence Brown (director); Frances Goodrich, Albert Hackett (screenwriters); Eugene O'Neill (playwright); Hunt Stromberg (producer).

Aladdin. 1992. Walt Disney Productions. Ron Clements, John Musker (directors, screenwriters, producers); Ted Elliott, Terry Rossio (screenwriters).

Alice in Wonderland. 1951. Walt Disney Productions. Clyde Geronimi, Wilfred Jackson, Hamilton Luske (directors); Lewis Carroll (novelist); Winston Hibler, Ted Sears, Bill Peet, Erdman Penner, Joe Rinaldi, Milt Banta, William Cottree, Dick Kelsey, Joe Grant, Dick Huemer, Del Connell, Tom Oreb, John Walbridge (screenwriters).

Anna Karenina. 1997. Warner Brothers/Icon Productions. Bernard Rose (director, screenwriter); Bruce Davey (producer); Jim Lemley (associate producer); Stephen McEveety (executive producer).

Anne of Green Gables. 1985. TV. TV-60 Film Produktion/Wonderworks/Canadian Broadcasting Corporation (CBC)/ City-TV/ Sullivan Entertainment, Inc. Kevin Sullivan (director, producer); Lucy Maud Montgomery (novelist); Ian McDougall (producer); Joe Wiesenfeld (screenwriter).

Awakenings. 1990. Columbia Pictures Corporation. Penny Marshall (director); Lawrence Lasker, Walter F. Parkes (producers); Amy Lemisch (associate producer); Steven Zaillean (screenwriter).

Awful Truth, The. 1937. Columbia Pictures Corporation. Leo McCarey, Vina Delmar (directors); W. Sidney Buchman (director, uncredited); Arthur Richman (playwright); Leo McCarey (producer); Everett Riskin (associate producer).

Beauty and the Beast. 1991. Walt Disney Productions. Gary Trousdale, Kirk Wise (directors); Linda Woolverton (screenwriter); Don Hahn (producer); Howard Ashman (executive producer); Sarah McArthur (associate producer).

"Beauty of Passage, The." Arens, N. Unpublished short story by UCLA School of Theater, Film and Television student.

Bionda, La (The Blonde). 1993. Sergio Rubini (director); W. Gian Filippo Ascianone, Umberto Marino, Sergio Rubini (screenwriters); Domanico Procacci, Fandango (producers).

Birdy. 1984. TriStar Pictures/A & M Films. Alan Parker (director); Jack

Behr, Sandy Kroopf (screenwriters); William Wharton (novelist); Ned Kopp (associate producer); David Manson (executive producer); Alan Marshall (producer).

Carousel. 1956. 20th Century Fox. Henry King (director); Ferenc Molnár (author of the play *Liliom*); Oscar Hammerstein II (book and lyrics); Benjamin F. Glazer (adaptation); Phoebe Ephron, Henry Ephron (screenwriters); Henry Ephron (producer).

Charlotte's Web. (E. B. White's *Charlotte's Web.*) 1973. Paramount Pictures. Charles A. Nichols, Iwao Takamoto (directors); Earl Hamner Jr. (screenwriter); E.B. White (novelist); Joseph Barbera, William Hanna (producers).

Children's Hour, The. 1961. United Artists/Mirisch Company. William Wyler (director, producer); John Michael Hayes (screenwriter); Lillian Hellman (playwright); Robert Wyler (producer).

City Hall. 1996. Columbia Pictures Corporation/Sony Pictures Classics. Harold Becker (director, producer); Bo Goldman, Nicholas Pileggi, Paul Schrader (screenwriters); Ken Lipper (screenwriter, producer); Charles Mulvehill, Edward R. Pressman (producers); Thomas J. Mack, Elizabeth Carroll (associate producers).

Climbing Fences. 1993. UCLA School of Theater, Film and Television student film by Mark Lawrence.

Color Purple, The. 1985. Warner Brothers/Amblin Entertainment/ Guber-Peters Company. Steven Spielberg (director, producer); Alice Walker (novelist); Menno Meyjes (screenwriter); Peter Guber, Jon Peters (executive producers); Carole Isenberg (associate producer); Quincy Jones, Kathleen Kennedy, Frank Marshall (producers).

Convicts. 1979. Unpublished play by H. Foote.

Cronaca di un Amore (Story of a Love Affair, The). 1950. Italy. Michelangelo Antonioni (director, screenwriter); Danielle D'Anza, Silvio Giovannetti, Francesco Maselli, Piéro Tellini (screenwriters); Villani Film, Stephano Caretta, Franco Villani (producers). (Based on *The Postman Always Rings Twice.*)

Dark-Adapted Eye, A. 1994. BBC. Tim Fywell (director); Ruth Rendell (novelist, as Barbara Vine); Sandy Welsh (screenwriter); Philipa Gates (producer).

Dead Man Walking. 1995. Working Title Films/Gramercy Pictures/ PolyGram Filmed Entertainment. Tim Robbins (director, screenwriter, producer); Sister Helen Prejean (author of the book); Tim Bevan, Eric Fellner (executive producers); Jon Kilik, Rudd Simmons (producers); Allan F. Nichols, Mark Seldis, Bob White (associate producers).

Dead Poets Society. 1989. Silver Screen Partners IV/Touchstone. Peter

Weir (director); Tom Schulman (screenwriter); Steven Haft, Paul
    Junger Witt, Tony Thomas (producers); Duncan Henderson (asso-
    ciate producer).

Death and the Maiden. 1994. Canal+ Productions/Channel Four Films
    (aka Film Four International) (aka Channel 4 TV [uk])/Fine Line/
    Flach Films/Kramer/Mount/TFI Films Productions (fr); Roman
    Polanski (director); Ariel Dorfman (screenwriter, co-producer);
    Rafael Yglesias (screenwriter); Jane Barclay, Sharon Marel (executive
    producers); Bonnie Timmermann (co-producer); Josh Kramer,
    Thom Mount (producers); Gladys Nederlander (associate producer).

"Dénouement." Rosenberg, J. Unpublished short story by UCLA School
    of Theater, Film and Television student.

Diary of Anne Frank, The. 1959. 20th Century Fox. George Stevens (di-
    rector, producer); Anne Frank (author of the diary); Frances
    Goodrich, Albert Hackett (screenwriters).

Dollhouse. 1994. UCLA School of Theater, Film and Television student
    film by Nicole Halpin.

Dreaming of Rope Ladders. Long, J.S. Unpublished play by UCLA School
    of Theater, Film and Television student.

Eating with Jude. 1997. UCLA School of Theater, Film and Television
    student film by Anne Kelly.

Emil and the Detectives. 1964. Walt Disney Productions/Buena Vista
    Television. Peter Tewksbury (director); A.J. Carothers (screen-
    writer); Erich Kaestner (novelist).

Emma. 1996. Haft Entertainment/Matchmaker Films/Miramax Films.
    Douglas McGrath (director, screenwriter); Jane Austen (novelist);
    Patrick Cassavetti, Steven Haft (producers); Donna Gigliotti, Bob
    Weinstein, Harvey Weinstein (executive producers); Donna Grey
    (associate producer).

Epiphany. Cores, L. Unpublished play, 70 East 10th Street, NY, NY 10003.

Fatal Beatings. 1994. Tiger Aspect Productions Ltd. John Howard
    Davies, Sue Vertue, Peter Bennett-Jones (producers).

Fisher King, The. 1991. Columbia Pictures Corporation. Terry Gilliam
    (director); Richard LaGravenese (screenwriter); Debra Hills, Lynda
    Obst (producers); Tony Mark, Stacey Sher (associate producers).

Fly Away Home. 1996. Columbia Pictures Corporation. Carroll Ballard
    (director); Bill Lishman (author of the autobiography); Vince
    McKewin, Robert Rodat (screenwriters); Carol Baum, John Veitch
    (producers); John M. Eckert (associate producer); Sandy Gallin (ex-
    ecutive producer).

Fools Rush In. 1997. Columbia Pictures Corporation. Andy Tennant (director); Joan Taylor (story); Katherine Reback (story, screenwriter); Anna Maria Davis (co-producer); Doug Draizin (producer); Michael McDonnell (executive producer); Steven P. Saeta (associate producer).

God Would Be Rich. Maley, Helen. 1996. Unpublished play. Box 185, West Tisbury, MA 02575.

Godfather III, The. 1990. Zoetrope Studios/Paramount Pictures. Francis Coppola (director, screenwriter, producer); Mario Puzo (screenwriter); Gray Frederickson, Charles Mulvehill, Fred Roos (co-producers); Fred Fuchs, Nicholas Gage (executive producers); Marina Gefter (associate producer).

Grapes of Wrath, The. 1940. 20th Century Fox. John Ford (director); Nunnally Johnson (screenwriter); John Steinbeck (novelist); Darryl F. Zanuck (producer).

Great Expectations. 1946. Cineguild. David Lean (director, screenwriter); Charles Dickens (novelist); Anthony Havelock-Allen (screenwriter, executive producer); Cecil McGivern, Kay Walsh (screenwriters); Ronald Neame (screenwriter, producer).

Henry IV, Parts I and II. 1979. TV. British Broadcasting Corporation (BBC)/Time-Life Television. David Giles (director); William Shakespeare (playwright); Cedric Messina (producer).

Hercules. 1997. Walt Disney Productions. Ron Clements, John Musker (directors, screenwriters, producers); John McEnery, Irene Mecchi, Bob Shaw (screenwriters); Barry Johnson (story); Alice Dewey (producer); Kendra Holland (associate producer).

Hunchback of Notre Dame, The. 1996. Walt Disney Productions. Gary Trousdale, Kirk Wise (directors); Victor Hugo (author of the novel *Notre Dame de Paris*); Irene Mecchi, Tab Murphy, Jonathan Roberts, Bob Tzudiker, Nona White (screenwriters); Roy Conli, Don Hahn (producers); Philip Lofaro (associate producer).

Hunger Waltz, The. Callaghan, S. Unpublished play by UCLA School of Theater, Film and Television student.

In Country. 1989. Warner Brothers/Yorktown Productions. Norman Jewison (director, producer); Bobbie Ann Mason (novelist); Cynthia Cidre, Frank Pierson (screenwriters); Richard Roth (producer); Michael Jewison (associate producer); Charles Mulvehill (executive producer).

In the Cemetary. 1994. Sandra Caruso (producer, director). From the one-woman dramatic presentation of *In Their Own Words: A Dramatic Series; Margaret Sanger: A Radiant Rebel*. Beverly Hills Television, Beverly Hills, CA 90212.

Inside. 1997. UCLA School of Theater, Film and Television student film by Mario Hernandez Jr.

Inventing the Abbotts. 1997. 20th Century Fox/Imagine Entertainment. Pat O'Connor (director); Sue Miller (novelist); Ken Hixon (story).

Jane Eyre. 1996. Miramax Films. Franco Zeffirelli (director, screenwriter); Charlotte Brontë (novelist); Hugh Whitemore (screenwriter); Guy East, Riccardo Tozzi (executive producers); Joyce Herlihy (associate producer); Jean Francois Lepetit, Giovannella Zannoni (co-producers); Dyson Lovell (producer); Bob Weinstein, Harvey Weinstein (co-executive producers).

Jesus of 148th Street. 1994. UCLA School of Theater, Film and Television student film by Timothy Martin Mills.

Joy Luck Club, The. 1993. Hollywood Pictures. Wayne Wang (director); Ronald Bass (screenwriter, producer); Amy Tan (screenwriter, novelist, producer); Patrick Markey (producer); Jessinta Liu Fung Ping (associate producer); Oliver Stone, Janet Yang (executive producers).

Kid, The. 1921. Chaplin—First National. Charles Chaplin (screenwriter, producer, director).

Killer, The. (Die xue shuang xiong.) 1989. Cantonese. Magnum Entertainment/Film Workshop Ltd./Golden Princess Film Production Limited. John Woo (director, screenwriter); Hark Tsui (producer).

Kiss Me Kate. 1953. MGM. George Sidney (director); Dorothy Kingsley, Sam Spewack, Bella Spewack (screenwriters); Cole Porter (playwright); Willam Shakespeare (playwright of *The Taming of the Shrew*); Jack Cummings (producer).

Lady Jane. 1986. Paramount Pictures. Trevor Nunn (director); Chris Bryant (story); David Edgar (screenwriter); Ted Lloyd (associate producer); Peter Snell (producer).

Language of Flowers, The. Villarreal, E. Unpublished play by UCLA School of Theater, Film and Television faculty member.

Life. Fincioen, Jake. Unpublished screenplay by UCLA School of Theater, Film and Television student.

Linda. 1997. UCLA School of Theater, Film and Television student film by Vivian Weisman.

Lion, the Witch, and the Wardrobe, The. (Aka *The Chronicles of Narnia: The Lion, the Witch, and the Wardrobe.*) Wonderworks/British Broadcasting Corporation. Marilyn Fox (director); C.S. Lewis (author of the novels); Alan Seymour (screenwriter); Colin Shindler (executive producer); Paul Stone (producer).

Little Princess, A. 1995. Warner Brothers/Baltimore Pictures. Alfonso

Cuarón (director); Frances Hodgson Burnett (novelist); Elizabeth Chandler, Richard LaGravenese (screenwriters); Alan C. Blomquist, Amy Ephron (executive producers); Dalisa Cohen (co-producer); Mark Johnson (producer).

Little Women. 1994. Columbia Pictures Corporation/DiNovi Pictures. Gillian Armstrong (director); Louisa May Alcott (novelist); Robin Swicord (screenwriter, co-producer); Warren Carr (associate producer); Denise DiNovi (producer).

Mambo Kings, The. 1992. Warner Brothers/Alcor Films/Le Studio Canal/Regency Enterprises. Arne Glimcher (director, producer); Oscar Hijuelos (novelist); Cynthia Cidre (screenwriter); Jack B. Bernstein (co-producer); Arnon Milchan (producer); Anna Reinhardt (associate producer); Steven Reuther (executive producer).

Men, Myths and Dogs. 1993. UCLA School of Theater, Film and Television student film by Anthony Pringle.

Midsummer Night's Dream, A. 1968. Peter Hall (director); William Shakespeare (playwright); Michael Birkett (producer).

Miracle Worker, The. 1962. Playfilm Productions. Arthur Penn (director); William Gibson (screenwriter, playwright); Helen Keller (author of *The Story of My Life*); Fred Coe (producer).

Misérables, Les. 1952. 20th Century Fox. Lewis Milestone (director); Victor Hugo (novelist); Richard Murphy (screenwriter); Fred Kohlmar (producer).

Much Ado About Nothing. 1993. British Broadcasting Corporation/Renaissance Films/Samuel Goldwyn Company. Kenneth Branagh (director, screenwriter, producer); William Shakespeare (playwright); Stephen Evans, David Parfitt (producers).

Nine Armenians. Ayvazian, L. Unpublished play. William Craver (agent); Writers & Artists, 19 West 44th Street, NY, NY 10036.

Of Mice and Men. 1992. Metro-Goldwyn-Mayer. Gary Sinise (director, producer); Horton Foote (screenwriter); John Steinbeck (novelist); Alan C. Blomquist, Russ Smith (producers).

Our Town. 1940. United Artists. Sam Woods (director); Harry Chandler, Frank Craven (screenwriters); Thornton Wilder (screenwriter; playwright); Sol Lesser (producer).

Parenthood. 1989. Universal Pictures. Ron Howard (director, screenwriter); Lowell Ganz, Babaloo Mandel (screenwriters); Brian Grazer (producer); Joseph M. Caracciolo Jr. (executive producer); Louisa Velis (associate producer).

Peter Pan. 1953. Walt Disney Productions. Clyde Geronimi, Wilfred Jackson, Hamilton Luske (directors); Milt Banta, William Cottrell, Winston Hibler, Bill Peet, Erdman Pener, Joe Rinaldi, Ted Sears, Ralph Wright (screenwriters); J.M. Barrie (playwright).

Pickwick Papers, The. 1952. Noel Langley (director, screenwriter); Charles Dickens (novelist); Bob McNaught (producer).

Pink Cookies. Taccone, Jorma. Unpublished play by UCLA School of Theater, Film and Television student.

Pippi Longstocking. (*Pippi Långstrump.*) 1997. Swedish. Trickompany/Beta Film/Nelvana Limited/TFC Trickompany GmbH/Iduna Film Productiongesellschaft /Svensk Filmindustri CSF/Téléfilm Canada. Bill Giggie (director, animation); Michael Schaack, Clive A. Smith (directors); Astrid Lindgren (novelist); Frank Nissen, Ken Sobol (additional dialogue); Waldemar Bergendahl, Hasmi Giakoumis, Merle-Anne Ridley (producers); David Ferguson (co-executive producer); Michael Hirsh, Patrick Loubert, Clive A. Smith (executive producers).

Pocahontas. 1995. Walt Disney Productions. Mike Gabriel, Eric Goldberg (directors); Carl Binder, Susannah Grant, Philip LaZebnik (screenwriters); Baker Bloodworth (associate producer); James Pentecost (producer).

Por Quinly Christmas, A. Long, Q. 1996. Unpublished play. Tantleff Agency, 375 Greenwich Street, Ste. 700, NY, NY 10013.

Postman Always Rings Twice, The. 1946. Tay Garnet (director); Niven Busch, Harry Ruskin (screenwriters); James M. Cain (novelist); Carey Wilson (producer).

Prime of Miss Jean Brodie, The. 1969. 20th Century Fox. Ronald Neame (director); Jay Presson Allen (screenwriter, playwright); Muriel Spark (novelist); Robert Fryer (producer).

Prince and the Pauper, The. Walt Disney Productions. George Scriber (director); Mark Twain (novelist); Dan Rounds (producer).

Proposals. Unpublished play by N. Simon.

Rebecca. 1940. Alfred Hitchcock (director); Daphne Du Maurier (novelist); Joan Harrison, Michael Hogan, Philip MacDonald, Robert E. Sherwood (screenwriters); David O. Selznick (producer).

Remains of the Day, The. 1993. Columbia Pictures Corporation/Merchant Ivory Productions. James Ivory (director); Kazuo Ishiguro (novelist); Ruth Prawer Jhabvala (screenwriter); John Calley, Ismail Merchant, Mike Nichols (producers); Paul Bradley (executive producer); Donald Rosenfeld (associate producer).

Rest of My Life, The. 1996. UCLA School of Theater, Film and Television student film by Mark Lawrence.

Richard III. 1995. United Artists/Bayly/Pare. Richard Loncraine (director, screenwriter); Ian McKellen (screenwriter, executive producer);

William Shakespeare (playwright); Maria Apodiacos, Ellen Dinerman Little, Joe Simon (executive producers); Stephen Bayly (producer); David Lascelles (line producer); Mary Richards, Michele Tandy (associate producers).

Schindler's List. 1993. Universal Pictures. Steven Spielberg (director, producer); Thomas Keneally (novelist); Steve Zaillian (screenwriter); Branko Lustig, Gerald R. Molen (producers); Lew Rywin (co-producer); Kathleen Kennedy (executive producer); Irving Glovin, Robert Raymond (associate producers).

Seagull, The. (Chaika.) 1970. Russian. Mosfilm. Yuli Karasik (director, screenwriter); Anton Chekhov (playwright).

Secret Garden, The. 1993. Warner Brothers/American Zoetrope. Agnieszka Holland (director); Frances Hodgson Burnett (novelist); Caroline Thompson (screenwriter, associate producer); Francis Coppola (executive producer); Fred Fuchs, Tom Luddy, Fred Roos (producers).

Secret of Roan Inish, The. 1994. Samuel Goldwyn/First Look Pictures. John Sayles (director, screenwriter); Rosalie K. Fry (novelist); Sarah Green, Maggie Renzi (producers); John Sloss, Peter Newman, Glenn R. Jones (executive producers); R. Paul Miller (associate producer).

Secret Santa. 1995. New York University Tisch School of the Arts student film by Matthew D. Huffman.

Shlemiel the First. Unpublished play. Adapted by R. Brustein from I. B. Singer's play.

Shiloh. 1997. Zeta Entertainment Ltd. Dale Rosenbloom (director, screenwriter, producer); Carl Borack (executive producer); Zane W. Levitt, Mark Yellen (producers).

Shop Around the Corner, The. 1940. MGM. Ernst Lubitsch (director, producer); Ben Hecht (screenwriter, uncredited); Nikolaus Laszlo (author of the play *Parfumerie*); Samson Raphaelson (screenwriter).

Sleepers. 1996. PolyGram Filmed Entertainment/Ascot Elite Entertainment Group/Warner Brothers. Barry Levinson (director, screenwriter, producer); Lorenzo Carcaterra (author of the book, co-producer); Steve Golin (producer); Peter Giuliano (executive producer); Gerrit Van der Meer (associate producer).

Sleepless in Seattle. 1993. TriStar. Nora Ephron (director, screenwriter); Jeff Arch, David S. Ward (screenwriters); Gary Foster (producer); Patrick Crowley, Lynda Obst (executive producers); Jane Bartelme, Delia Ephron, James W. Skotchdopole (associate producers).

Sling Blade. 1996. Shooting Gallery Films/Miramax. Billy Bob Thornton (director and screenwriter); David L. Bushell, Brandon Rosser (producers); Larry Meistrich (executive producer).

Slow Dance. 1997. UCLA School of Theater, Film and Television student film by Carl Pfirman.

Something Is Missing. Staab, J. Unpublished play by Wheelock College faculty member. 200 The Riverway, Boston, MA 02215.

Stage Door. 1937. RKO Radio Pictures. Gregory LaCava (director); Edna Ferber, George S. Kaufman (playwrights); Morrie Ryskind, Anthony Veiller (screenwriters); Pandro S. Berman (producer).

Stationmaster's Wife, The. (Bolweiser.) 1977. West German. Bavaria Atelier. Rainer Werner Fassbinder (director, screenwriter); Oskar Maria Graf (screenwriter); Herbert Knopp (producer).

Steel Magnolias. 1989. TriStar. Herbert Ross (director); Robert Harling (playwright); Ray Stark (producer); Andrew Stone (associate producer); Victoria White (executive producer).

Swingers. 1996. Alfred Shay Company, Inc./Miramax. Doug Liman (director); Jon Farreau (screenwriter, co-producer); Victor Simpkins (producer); Cary Woods (executive producer); Avram Ludwig, Bradford L. Schlei (associate producers); Nicole LaLoggia (line).

Taming of the Shrew, The. 1980. TV. British Broadcasting Corporation/ Time-Life Television. Jonathan Miller (director, producer); William Shakespeare (playwright).

To Kill a Mockingbird. 1962. Universal International/Pakula-Mulligan, Brentwood Productions. Robert Mulligan (director); Harper Lee (novelist); Horton Foote (screenwriter); Alan J. Pakula (producer).

To Play the King. 1994. Miniseries. British Broadcasting Corporation. Paul Seed (director); Andrew Davies (screenwriter); Michael Dobbs (novelist); Ken Riddington (producer).

Tom Sawyer. 1995. Walt Disney Productions/Painted Fence Productions. Peter Hewitt (director); Ron Koslow, David Loughery, Stephen Sommers (screenwriters); Mark Twain (novelist); John Baldecchi, Laurence Mark (producers); Barry Bernardi (executive producer).

Tous les Matins du Monde. (All the Mornings of the World). 1991. France. Paravision Int. S.A./D.D. Productions. Alain Corneau (director, screenwriter); Pascal Quignard (screenwriter); Bernard Marescot (producer).

Tumbleweeds, The. Ham, C. Unpublished play by UCLA School of Theater, Film and Television student.

Twelfth Night, or What You Will. 1996. Renaissance Films/Summit Entertainment. Trevor Nunn (director, screenwriter); William Shakespeare (playwright); Mark Cooper (line producer); Stephen Evans, David Parfitt (producers); Ileen Maisel, Greg Smith, Ruth Vitale, Jonathan Weisgal (executive producers).

Uncle Tom's Cabin. 1927. Silent. Universal Pictures (aka MCA/Universal Pictures). Harry A. Pollard (director); Harriet Beecher Stowe (novelist).

Waterland. 1992. United Kingdom. Channel Four Films (aka Film Four International). Stephen Gyllenhaal (director); Graham Swift (novelist); Peter Prince (screenwriter); Patrick Cassavetti, Katy McGuinness (producers); Ira Deutchman, Nik Powell, Stephen Woolley (executive producers).

Wind in the Willows, The. (US video title *Mr. Toad's Wild Ride.*) 1996. Allied Filmmakers. Terry Jones (director, screenwriter); Kenneth Grahame (novelist); Jake Eberts, John Goldstone (producers).

Winnie-the-Pooh. (*The Many Adventures of Winnie The Pooh.*) 1977. Walt Disney Productions. John Lounsbery, Wolfgang Reitherman (directors); Ken Anderson, Xavier Arencio, Ted Berman, Larry Clemmons, Eric Cleworth, Vance Gerry, Winston Hibler, Julius Svendsen (screenwriters); Ralph Wright (story); A.A. Milne (author of the novels); Wolfgang Reitherman (producer).

Winter Sun. Grignon, W. Unpublished screenplay by UCLA School of Theater, Film and Television student.

Wizard of Oz, The. 1939. MGM. George Cukor (director, test scenes, uncredited); Victor Fleming (director); Richard Thorpe (director, original scenes, uncredited); King Vidor (director, Kansas scenes, uncredited); L. Frank Baum (novelist); Noel Langley, Florence Ryerson, Edgar Allan Woolf (screenwriters); Irving Brecher, William H. Cannon, Herbert Fields, Arthur Freed, Jack Haley, E.Y. Harburg, Samuel Hoffenstein, Bert Lahr, John Lee Mahin, Herman J. Mankiewicz, Jack Mintz, Ogden Nash, Sid Silvers (uncredited screenwriters); Mervyn LeRoy (producer).

All inquiries regarding unpublished manuscripts, unreleased films, and unpublished short stories by UCLA School of Theater, Film and Television faculty or students should be directed to: UCLA, School of Theater, Film and Television, 102 East Melnitz, 405 North Hilgard Avenue, Los Angeles, CA 90024-1622.

INDEX